The Streamliner Diner Cookbook

▪THE▪
Streamliner Diner
▪COOKBOOK▪

Alexandra Rust, Elizabeth Matteson,
Judith Weinstock, and Irene Clark

ILLUSTRATED BY
Irene Clark

1〇 TEN SPEED PRESS
Berkeley, California

TO ALL OUR RELATIONS

🔟

TEN SPEED PRESS
P.O. Box 7123
Berkeley, California 94707

Cover and interior illustrations by Irene Clark
Cover and text design by Nancy Austin
Composition by Wilsted & Taylor, Oakland, California

Library of Congress Cataloging-in-Publication Data

The Streamliner Diner cookbook / Alexandra Rust . . . [et al.].
    Includes index.   p.   cm.
    ISBN 0-89815-378-6
    1. Cookery, American.   2. Streamliner Diner (Restaurant)—History.
I. Rust, Alexandra.   II. Streamliner Diner (Restaurant)
TX715.S9   1990
641.5973—dc20   90-42367
                                                                                          CIP

First printing, 1990

5   4   3   2   1   –   94   93   92   91   90

Manufactured in the United States of America

ACKNOWLEDGEMENTS

To Ten Speed Press for saying yes!

To Jackie Wan for her expertise, patience, insight, good humor, succinct style, and excellent editing.

To Allan and Gloria Patterson for encouraging us from the very beginning.

To our committed tasting crew: Chris Witkowski, Linda Hunt, Frank Converse, Morgan Andersen, Stefanie Van Tacky, Michael Gibson, George Little, B. Susan Johnson, Kimara Sajn, Jeffrey Bodony, Devin, Sarah Favret, John Steiner, Julie Clifford, Colette Arcand, Michael Rust, Orion Brown, Damien Wayne, Neil Tennyson, and Gloria and Allan Patterson.

To our managers, Stef and Julie, for helping us keep it all together.

To our staff, for keeping the restaurant full of good smells and humor, even when the omelette hits the fan.

To our customers, from all walks of life.

To our suppliers, for keeping us well stocked with food and supplies.

To Julie Storey and Leigh Ann Giles, who started the tradition of streamliner down-home gourmet food.

To Beth Johnson, for sharing with us five years of cooking, managing, endless insights, continuous support, incredible recipes, a voracious appetite for eating fine food and reading cookbooks, and last but not least, her friendship.

To Liz's family: Rick, Susie, and Daidie who helped critique the writing; and Jane, Bob, Caitlin, Sean, Summer, Rob, Uncle Sumner, Elliot, and Owen.

To Alex's family: Michael, Damien, Orion, Mom, and Dad. To Irene's family: Marca, Cosmo, and the entire Clark clan. To Judith's family: David, Devin, Samuel, and the entire Johnson clan for their love of good food.

CONTENTS

FOREWORD

Impressions of the Diner

I've been a patron of the Streamliner Diner since it opened; but I don't like its name. It's cute but misleading. Implied in the word *streamliner* is one of those stainless steel, chrome, glass-and-neon urban nostalgia creations; statement rather than substance. The Diner is just the opposite. It's food and people and feelings; substance which, for a regular patron, is experienced as a patchwork quilt of savory experiences and warm relationships. Once you try the tasty and wholesome recipes in this book, you will understand how the food contributes toward patron loyalty; so let me dwell on what else makes the Diner special to us regulars.

On Bainbridge Island, at the west end of a thirty-five-minute ferry ride across Puget Sound from Seattle, the Diner sits on the east end of a stark 1950s concrete-block-and-board one-story building on the main street of Winslow, a town with the overinflated designation of "city." The restaurant shares the building with a beauty parlor and a real estate office. The Diner has the proportions of two shoe boxes stacked on top of one another. The front is all glass, and the east side is mostly so. That's good, because breakfasts are a big deal, especially on a weekend, and the morning sun enhances the experience.

Timing your arrival is important on summer weekends. Patrons from Seattle descend in massive waves set by the scheduled trips of the ferries across Puget Sound; so wise Bainbridge Islanders either line up before the 8:00 A.M. opening or slot later breakfasts into the gaps between ferry dockings.

Once through the door, the patron inhales the fragrance of coffee, bacon, and whatever herbs and spices are going into the specials of the day. Despite the high ceiling, the clatter of dishes and silverware and the echoing rumble of closely confined conversations almost drown out the music. Depending on who's cooking behind the long counter running lengthwise down the center, the latter may be folk, classical, golden oldies, soft rock, or jazz.

While eight tables (plus two on an outdoor deck in the summer) provide room to spread out the Sunday paper or study the latest art or craft works hung on the walls, the counter stools are more involving. Most often starring at the grill are one of the four owners. Typically, on weekends it's either Liz or Alex. I seem to catch performances by Irene or Judith more often on weekdays.

In a space about equal to six telephone booths in a row, each prima ballerina of the grill works with one or two other food preparers in supporting roles. Besides keeping the grillmistress supplied, the latter heat quiches and pastries in the ovens, or later in the day slice, grind, mix, and bake what must be prepared ahead for the next day's meals. Weaving through these close confines are two waitpersons and one or two scullery help. Particularly when the heat of a summer sun sets me to perspiring on the cool side of the counter, I am awed that so many, faces ruddy and glistening from heat of grill, oven, and dishwasher, can work so swiftly, effectively, and goodnaturedly in such close confines.

Since I have managed people and serve as a consultant on working relationship problems, I appreciate the importance of leadership by example and the selection of good people. The four partners have a knack for both. Despite the hubbub and lines of people waiting to be seated, each works in a state of moving meditation, resembling a serene ballerina. Not a motion is wasted. Looking over her shoulder, I see dark bread popped out of the toaster just in time to serve as a platform for poached eggs surmounted by sautéed spinach and mushrooms. Meanwhile omelettes, jam-packed with meats, cheeses, and vegetables, have been carefully turned, chunky home fries flipped, and several bubbling eggs miraculously "once-overed" without bursting. The quiet concentration is emulated by the other food preparers and the scullery staff.

Pivoting on my stool, I can enjoy the different performance of the waitpersons. They quickstep out from behind the cash register, down the narrow corridor between tables and counter to the front door (and out on the deck in the summer), dispensing steaming plates, coffee, and continual conversation in a swirling reel with arriving and departing patrons and wandering children. Like their associates behind the counter, they waste not a motion, pausing to relax only when the tides of customers have slackened. Natural breaks occur while the latest boatload of diners are savoring their meals. Then Liz may massage Alex's shoulders while they face about and chat with those of us in the audience lucky enough to be on counter stools.

On weekdays, mid-morning or afternoon, especially on a rainy winter's day, when windows are moist with steam, the Diner may be nearly empty. Then staff can take time to visit with patrons, and the latter learn that one is a painter, another has a master's degree in economics, another is a weaver, another is a punk rocker, yet another is a poet, and one is actually a ballet dancer. Their spouses, friends, children, or parents drop in and get introduced. When we bring ours in we reciprocate.

It gradually dawns on us, regular patrons and staff, with all our diverse backgrounds, that we have become members of a unique institution, expressing the values of four strong, thoughtful women in the presentation and enjoyment of both good, healthy food and mutually respectful fellowships. May it last.

—Allan G. Patterson

INTRODUCTION

People who have never been here always want to know what makes the Stream-liner Diner a *diner*. They picture a converted railway dining car with flashy neon signs and a chrome exterior. The fact is: sorry, no chrome exterior, no dining car, no Formica or Naugahyde, and no jukebox. The counter is laminated oak and the floors are carpeted. The bar stools are upholstered in dusty rose velveteen, and the tables are draped with colorful 1950s tablecloths bearing images of flowers, fruit, and maps of Florida. Not exactly diner decor.

Our food is not typical diner food, either. No "real" diner would serve roast beef sandwiches with alfalfa sprouts or gourmet coffee instead of "joe." We do. A "real" diner would have grilled cheese sandwiches, canned soup, or pork chops on the menu. We don't. But we do serve some favorite traditionals, like Friday Meat Loaf or Dad's Chicken Pot Pie. And we do offer basic breakfast combinations like eggs-bacon-waffle, eggs-links-toast, etc., although we go off the beaten track more often than not.

Still, the Streamliner Diner is decidedly a diner. For one thing, it's shaped like one. It's long and narrow, and so small that it only holds eight tables. Stretching most of the length of the dining area is a counter with ten bar stools overlooking the kitchen, which is also long and narrow. The bar stools seat total strangers next to each other. More than anything else, this closeness is what gives the Diner a true "diner" feel. Customers befriend each other and end up discussing politics or local housing prices while they watch the cooks preparing their meals. The cooks and other staff take part in these conversations freely, too.

The dynamics of the Diner are ever-changing, depending on who is present. Carpenters come for lunch breaks, families bring their small children, and friends get together over breakfast. Others come to network and rendezvous or hold business meetings. Locals bring us flowers, island gossip, and weather reports. Some of our "regulars" flatter us by coming in twice a day. Over time, we have established strong bonds with many of the customers who frequent our place.

The four of us who now own the Streamliner Diner all worked as cooks for the original owners. When we learned of their intent to sell, we decided to go into partnership, buy the diner, and run the place ourselves. We have been owners since 1985. We all still take our turns as regularly scheduled cooks, and on the days that we cook, we also manage the restaurant. We've found that overseeing the kitchen, cooking, and managing the entire place simultaneously is a monumental task, especially on busy days. This experience has taught us that we could not possibly run the business without each other. Not only have we survived for six years in this four-way partnership, but our relationship has flourished and continues to grow stronger.

Besides helping to bear the work load, we each contribute complementary skills and strengths to the partnership . . .

■　　　■　　　■

Irene has single-handedly created the artistic ambience of the Streamliner Diner. People come from miles around to enjoy their food among her seasonal bouquets and the quirky little knickknacks that she's found in out-of-the-way secondhand stores. She has turned the walls into a gallery, arranging monthly shows for talented local artists. To the kitchen she contributes her foragings of mushrooms, watercress, clams, and oysters as special treats. The blackberries, huckleberries, and plums she picks enhance our coffee cakes, kuchen, and kugels in summer. Irene is also an excellent cook and has a distinct style all her own with many of the dishes she prepares.

Her copious talents are enhanced by her humorous, generous, and heartfelt presence. She tends to our employees like a mother hen tends to her chicks, with a well-placed peck or two when needed. Her experience with chicks comes from raising two children who are now young adults and have followed in their mother's footsteps. Cosmo, like his mom, knows that fishing and foraging surpass shopping. Her daughter, Marca, is an artist and a good cook in her own right. She has graced the Streamliner Diner with her good cooking in the summertime.

Irene is an island old-timer, not in age, but in ability to "hang out with the boys" and carry on an all-star bull session. Her star quality is being able to cross all lines of age, sex, language, and humor. She touches people in a way that pulls them in and makes them want to linger a little longer.

■   ■   ■

Judith can grasp a concept and bring it to completion faster than spinning around twice. There is no job or obstacle that ever daunts her. A study in calmness amidst perpetual motion, Judith's life amazes all who know her. The number of projects that she adeptly juggles is a wonder to her associates. From our telling, she might sound like a Type A personality. However, she puts us at ease with her reassuring attitude, calm demeanor, and radiant smile. The only thing high-strung about Judith is her twelve-string guitar.

Coming from a large family has given her expertise in interacting with people. She has instigated holiday feasts at the Streamliner Diner for those without family in the area and works to create a familial camaraderie in the kitchen.

As a creative, improvisational cook, Judith has contributed delectable masterpieces such as Kahlua Cream Pie, Orange Pumpkin Honey Muffins, Tomato Herb Braid, Italian Poached Fish, and many other fabulous dishes. Her refreshingly uninhibited wild spirit echoes in her cooking style. She has an innate sense of how foods and seasonings go together. She is fearless except when forced to measure things. Her frustration as she had to measure ingredients to prepare recipes for this cookbook was comic relief in the tedium of teaspoons and cups. She reads cookbooks like some people read *House Beautiful* magazine, gleaning ideas, but never using a recipe to cook. She is able to accomplish great tasks, making them appear effortless. Like the man on the flying trapeze, she flies through the air with the greatest of ease.

Besides being a whiz in the kitchen, she has also kept our books together for five years. Judith's previous business experience includes having been a partner in two collective restaurants. She is also a member of We Three, a women's a cappella group that has performed up and down the West Coast for the past ten years. Judith and her husband, David, have included the Streamliner as an integral part of numerous peace benefits in the Seattle area. She is the mother of two messy, loveable young children, Devin and Sam.

■   ■   ■

If our partnership had been formed in prehistoric times, Alexandra would have been the one to invent the wheel. When we bought the Streamliner Diner, only one of us had experience in the restaurant business. We had no management experience and were four nice women in the jaws of an historically not-so-nice business. We had the pieces of a grand beginning when we took over, and Alex has led the way in overall improvement of management practices, upgrading of equipment, and finding the delicate balance between traditionally female accommodation and male assertiveness. She is not afraid to ask for what is needed. This can be scary to most women, and we were in need of this particular skill. She balances it with a relaxed vulnerability when the situation demands. Alex has persisted, and is finally winning us over to good business practices that don't always attract popular response but are smart internal disciplines. In short, she takes control of the situation with competence and clear thinking.

She pays attention to the finer details that seem insignificant but that add up to huge savings in time, money, and energy. She has prodded us to define and write up manuals and job descriptions for our employees. She figured out that we could pay for a new ice machine in seven months with the savings we would accrue by not shopping for ice at the local supermarket. She has also inexhaustibly and without complaint negotiated for everything from waffle iron parts and honey pourers to carpet and plates.

Wherever she goes, Alex has a knack for noticing what makes other restaurants successful and inviting. She brings this awareness to us and to her cooking. When she experiences a wonderful dish at a friend's house or at an ethnic restaurant, she eagerly tries to recreate it for the Streamliner Diner.

Such experimenting has resulted in her own luscious versions of Fillo Rustica and Coastal Shrimp and Crab Gumbo. Alex delights in making a superb rendition of her grandmother's kolaches. Besides her good cooking and business skills, Alex brings consistent good humor in the wee hours of the morn and always has time for a customer that has gotten used to an attentive ear.

Alex has another full-time job as the mother of two sons, Damian and Orion, who have both washed a dish or two at the Streamliner Diner. In addition, she is a botany student at the University of Washington. Among her many passions in life are her roses, her fiddle, and her husband, Michael. She still finds time for fiddle stomping as she plays to her dog, Reuben, who howls off-key, and she's working on getting in a few dances with Michael.

■   ■   ■

In our 4 × 12-foot pencil-shaped kitchen, every aspect of food preparation is in open view to the customers. To look at the amazed countenances of those seated at the counter on the weekends, one would imagine they were watching a three-ring circus or a fascinating musical. But no, they are the captivated audience of the one and only "Grill Wonder," otherwise known as Elizabeth, the Grill Queen. Our patrons gape as she nonchalantly juggles four omelettes, one quiche, two specials, four waffles, and a #87. She can single-handedly feed 200 people aesthetically pleasing, melt-in-your-mouth breakfasts in the course of one morning. In every group there are roles to fill, and each person, if it is a successful partnership, finds his or her niche. In our tiny kitchen, high-stress situations often arise. Liz has taken on the role of listener and mediator in these circumstances, always being there to nonthreateningly hear both sides. She seems tentative when you first meet her, but watch out! She is one of the strongest women we know, emotionally as well as physically. As you sit at the counter and watch her feed the hungry hordes, or run up a mile-long hill with her (on the eighteenth mile), or listen to her query about the demands of human relationships, you can forget she has limits. One of Liz's strong points is that she allows you to see her limits, and she helps those around her to define theirs. This is a subtle, simple gift that helps make our restaurant a more humane place to work. Liz is invaluable in our cramped little diner. She has organized our upstairs nightmare of bulk foods and our never-quite-secure schedule in the kitchen. She undertook the task of planning our first out-of-shop job last spring. That consisted of organizing food ordering, staffing, and facility design and equipment for the Seattle Folklife Festival, an event which annually attracts tens of thousands of people.

We have dubbed her the Grill Queen, but her skills reach far beyond the flipping of eggs. In her not-so-spare time, Liz helps to organize the summer Audubon program for children in the Seattle area. She is in her element groping in tide pools, hiking in the forest, and identifying constellations on midnight walks. Aren't we lucky she manages that 4:30 A.M. grill call?

Though Lizzie is our ruling monarch on the grill, everyone on our kitchen staff learns to be a grill cook. And that is true of most areas of food preparation here. We have no *sauciers*, bakers, or "pastry chefs." All the cooks know how to make bagels, pies, soups, quiches, entrées, and salads. In fact, some cooks wait tables and some dishwashers cook. Of course, a cook or chef will be better at one thing than another, but we have no experts. Our survival and success have hinged on the staff's versatility and broad expertise rather than on individual specialization.

To say that our kitchen is challenging is a gross understatement. There are usually three cooks in the tiny kitchen at a time. Since the floor space averages three feet in width, you have to turn sideways to get around another person. Rare is the occasion when you can walk from one end of the kitchen to the other facing forward.

Counter space and cooling places for baked goods are just as limited. When we are baking, we have pans stacked all over the place. Customers seem amused as we try to find a cooling spot for that last muffin tin that just came out of the oven.

We receive staggered deliveries all week long from food distributors in Seattle. Keep in mind that all these deliveries come in right through the front door, since that is our only door. Box after box rides in on dollies through the slender dining area during busy lunches and breakfasts for a little added chaos.

The lack of storage space and refrigeration space together with the reality of living on an island definitely restrict us and affect our menu planning. We don't have room for ten varieties of exotic meats and cheese. You will find that most of the ingredients we use are quite ordinary and readily available at the average grocery store. In fact we purchase some of our food at retail prices at our local supermarket simply because we can't store large amounts of food.

The seasons and local harvest are also a factor in determining what goes on the menu. We have several local gardeners and farmers who sell us organic produce. Although our customers have not expressed an overwhelming preference for organic foods, we prefer them, and if the prices are comparable to those of their nonorganic counterparts, we will choose the organic.

Our style of cooking might best be described as down-home gourmet cooking. Everything is made from scratch, and we pride ourselves on the care that goes into all the dishes we serve in our restaurant. We prepare foods as we would like them to taste and have learned to trust our intuitions when it comes to cooking.

We do not consider ourselves inventors, for the most part, and few of our recipes are truly original. We do like to experiment, though, and feel free to mix the colors of our palette as we are inspired. As a result, our menus are unusually eclectic. Lunch could be oriental one day, and Mexican the next; East Indian the third day, and Cajun the fourth. Our regulars have to be a flexible lot!

Since none of us has had formal culinary training, the rules governing what constitutes "true" French cuisine or "authentic" Italian food do not apply. Our loyal clientele has come to expect and appreciate this "streamlining" of classic dishes. And after all is said and done, our main object is to please our patrons. Their willingness to try new dishes and the pleasure they take in the food we set before them is the fuel that nourishes our creativity.

For those who know and love the Streamliner Diner, here are the recipes you have been patiently awaiting. For those who have never visited our diner on Bainbridge Island, the drawings, recipes, and anecdotes in this book will help to evoke an image of the Streamliner Diner life and food. We heartily invite you to experiment with the recipes in this cookbook. So put on your apron, sharpen your knife, and fire up the stove!

TABLE OF MEASURES

1 dash	=	6 drops
1 tablespoon	=	3 teaspoons
2 tablespoons	=	1 fluid ounce
4 tablespoons	=	¼ cup
1 cup	=	8 fluid ounces or ½ pint
1 quart	=	2 pints
1 gallon	=	4 quarts or 128 fluid ounces

TABLE OF EQUIVALENTS

apples	1 medium-sized	1 cup grated
basil	4 ounces	2 cups leaves, packed
berries	6 ounces	1 cup
bread crumbs, dry	⅓ cup	1 slice
butter	1 pound	2 cups
	¼ pound	8 tablespoons
celery	1 stalk	⅓ cup chopped
cheese,		
cream	8 ounces	1 cup
freshly grated	1 pound	5 cups
ricotta	1 15-ounce container	2 cups
cream,		
whipping	1 cup	2 cups whipped
flour	1 pound	4 cups
lemons	1 medium-sized	2 to 4 tablespoons juice, 1 tablespoon zest
mushrooms	1 pound	6 cups chopped
noodles	8 ounces dry	4 cups cooked

onions	1 medium-sized	1 cup chopped
oranges	1 medium-sized	6 to 8 tablespoons juice, 2 to 3 tablespoons zest
peppers, green	1 medium-sized	1 cup chopped
pine nuts	5 ounces	1 cup whole, $\frac{2}{3}$ cup chopped
polenta	1 cup dry	3 cups cooked
potatoes	1 medium-sized	1 cup chopped
raisins	1 pound	$2\frac{3}{8}$ cups
rhubarb	1 pound	4 cups sliced
rice	2 cups raw	5 cups cooked
squash	$2\frac{1}{2}$ pounds	3 cups cooked and mashed
strawberries	1 pound	3 cups sliced
sugar,		
granulated	1 pound	2 cups
brown	1 pound	$2\frac{1}{4}$ cups packed
tomatoes	1 medium-sized	1 cup chopped

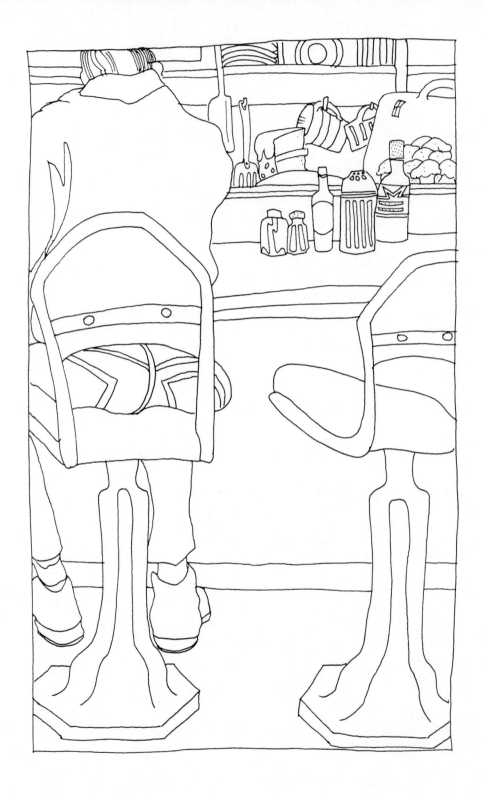

MUFFINS

A new crop of freshly baked muffins emerges from our ovens daily. We make so many that our muffin trays fill up every available surface in the kitchen while the muffins cool. It's muffin mania!

We mix the batter in large soup pots and refrigerate it overnight. When we come in the next morning, all we have to do is grease the muffin tins (the standard three-inch size), spoon in the batter (all the way to the top), and pop them into the oven.

Our muffins are sweet, but not overly so. Most of them are made with honey or maple syrup instead of sugar. We also have several dairy-free recipes, such as the Carrot Spice Muffins and the Apricot Pineapple Muffins.

Muffins make a great quick breakfast and also pack well in lunches. They are rewarding travelling companions on trips and picnics. Many commuters on the way to Seattle stop by the Diner regularly just to grab a muffin for breakfast.

Peanut Butter Muffins

¼ cup butter or margarine

2 cups unbleached white flour
1 teaspoon baking powder
1 teaspoon baking soda
¼ cup granulated sugar
½ cup brown sugar
½ teaspoon salt

2 large eggs, beaten
1 cup buttermilk
⅔ cup chunky peanut butter
2 teaspoons vanilla

Preheat oven to 350°. Grease muffin tins. Melt the butter or margarine and let cool.

Mix all the dry ingredients in a medium-sized bowl. In another medium-sized bowl, whisk the eggs, buttermilk, peanut butter, vanilla, and melted butter.

Make a well in the middle of the dry ingredients. Add wet ingredients and mix with as few strokes as possible. Don't overmix. Spoon the batter into the muffin tins. Bake at 350° for 20 minutes.

Yield: 10 muffins

Maple Nut Muffins

¼ cup butter or margarine

2 cups unbleached white flour

1 teaspoon baking soda

1 teaspoon baking powder

½ teaspoon salt

¾ cup walnuts, toasted and finely chopped

2 large eggs, beaten

¾ cup maple syrup

½ cup buttermilk

2 teaspoons vanilla

Preheat oven to 350°. Grease muffin tins. Melt butter or margarine. Let cool.

Mix the flour, baking soda, baking powder, salt, and walnuts in a medium-sized bowl. In another medium-sized bowl, whisk together all wet ingredients, including the melted butter or margarine.

Make a well in the middle of the dry ingredients. Add wet ingredients and mix with as few strokes as possible. Don't overmix. Spoon batter into muffin tins. Bake at 350° for 15 to 20 minutes, until light brown on top. These muffins dry out quickly if overbaked.

Yield: 9 muffins

Bran Oatmeal Muffins

1 cup boiling water
1 cup bran
½ cup butter or margarine

2½ cups unbleached white flour
2 cups rolled oats
½ teaspoon salt
2½ teaspoons baking soda
1 cup raisins
zest of 1 orange

1 cup honey
2 large eggs, beaten
1 cup buttermilk
⅔ cup orange juice concentrate

Preheat oven to 375°. Grease muffin tins. In a small bowl, pour boiling water over the bran and let sit 5 minutes. Melt the butter or margarine and let cool.

In a large bowl, mix the flour, oats, salt, baking soda, raisins, and zest. In a medium-sized bowl, whisk together the bran, melted butter, honey, eggs, buttermilk, and orange juice concentrate.

Make a well in the middle of the dry ingredients. Add wet ingredients and mix with as few strokes as possible. Don't overmix. Spoon batter into muffin tins. Bake for 20 to 25 minutes at 375° until the muffins are brown and spring back when touched.

Yield: 16 muffins

VARIATIONS

- Add up to 1 cup of any of the following ingredients to the dry ingredients: nuts, cranberries, blueberries, grated carrots, coconut, or drained crushed pineapple.

- Add ½ teaspoon almond extract or 1 teaspoon vanilla extract to the wet mix, or 1 teaspoon cinnamon to the dry ingredients.

Seed and Nut Muffins
(See Da Nut Muffins)

½ cup butter or margarine

¼ cup shredded coconut

2 tablespoons sesame seeds

2 tablespoons sunflower seeds

2 tablespoons pine nuts

2 tablespoons chopped almonds

1½ cups unbleached white flour

¾ cup whole wheat flour

¼ cup bran

½ cup rolled oats

½ teaspoon cardamom

1 teaspoon baking powder

1 teaspoon baking soda

½ teaspoon salt

2 large eggs, beaten

¾ cup honey

¾ cup buttermilk

½ teaspoon almond extract

Preheat oven to 350°. Grease muffin tins. Melt the butter or margarine and let cool. Toast the coconut, seeds, and nuts in a 350° oven for 4 to 5 minutes. Cool.

Combine the flours, bran, oats, cardamom, baking powder, baking soda, and salt in a large bowl. Add the coconut, seeds, and nuts, and mix well. In another bowl, whisk the melted butter or margarine, eggs, honey, buttermilk, and almond extract.

Make a well in the middle of the dry ingredients. Add wet ingredients and mix with as few strokes as possible. Don't overmix. Spoon batter into muffin tins. Bake at 350° for 20 to 25 minutes.

Yield: 1 dozen muffins

Apricot Pineapple Muffins

½ cup dried apricots

¼ cup raisins

½ cup apple juice

1 tablespoon lemon juice

¼ cup butter or margarine

⅓ cup rolled oats

3 cups unbleached white flour

1 teaspoon salt

1½ teaspoons baking soda

2 large eggs, beaten

½ cup honey

½ teaspoon almond extract

1 cup cooked cereal (8-grain or oatmeal)

1¼ cups canned crushed pineapple

Soak the apricots and raisins in apple and lemon juice for 1 hour. Drain and reserve the juice for the batter. Coarsely chop the fruit.

Preheat oven to 350°. Grease muffin tins. Melt the butter or margarine and let cool.

Mix all the dry ingredients in a large bowl. In another bowl, whisk together the chopped fruit, reserved fruit juice, butter or margarine, eggs, honey, almond extract, cereal, and pineapple.

Make a well in the middle of the dry ingredients. Add wet ingredients and mix with as few strokes as possible. Don't overmix. Spoon batter into muffin tins. Bake at 350° for 25 minutes.

Yield: 16 muffins

Graham Coconut Muffins

¼ cup butter or margarine

2 cups unbleached white flour
¾ cup grated coconut
¾ cup graham cracker crumbs
¾ cup brown sugar
1 teaspoon baking soda
1 teaspoon baking powder
½ teaspoon salt

2 large eggs, beaten
1¼ cups buttermilk
2 teaspoons vanilla

Preheat oven to 350°. Grease muffin tins. Melt the butter or margarine and let cool.

Mix all the dry ingredients in a medium-sized bowl, including the coconut. In another medium-sized bowl, whisk all wet ingredients, including the melted butter or margarine.

Make a well in the middle of the dry ingredients. Add wet ingredients and mix with as few strokes as possible. Don't overmix. Spoon batter into muffin tins. Bake at 350° for 20 minutes.

Yield: 10 muffins

Carrot Spice Muffins

½ cup butter or margarine

2 cups unbleached white flour
1 teaspoon baking powder
1 teaspoon baking soda
½ teaspoon salt
1 teaspoon cinnamon
1⅓ cups grated carrots
⅔ cup walnuts, chopped
⅓ cup raisins

2 large eggs, beaten
1 cup honey
½ teaspoon vanilla

Preheat oven to 350°. Grease muffin tins. Melt the butter or margarine and let cool.

In a medium-sized bowl, combine the flour, baking powder, baking soda, salt, and cinnamon. Add the carrots, walnuts, and raisins and mix thoroughly.

In a small bowl, whisk together the melted butter, eggs, honey, and vanilla.

Make a well in the middle of the dry ingredients. Add wet ingredients and mix with as few strokes as possible. Don't overmix. Spoon batter into muffin tins. Bake at 350° for 25 to 30 minutes.

Yield: 10 muffins

Lemon Sour Cream Muffins

½ cup butter or margarine

2 cups unbleached white flour

1 cup sugar

½ teaspoon salt

1 teaspoon baking soda

2 teaspoons baking powder

2 large eggs, beaten

1 cup sour cream

¼ cup lemon juice

zest and juice of 1 lemon

Preheat oven to 350°. Grease muffin tins. Melt the butter or margarine and let cool.

Thoroughly mix all the dry ingredients in a large bowl. Whisk together the eggs and sour cream in a smaller bowl. Stir in the butter or margarine, ¼ cup lemon juice, and zest and juice of lemon.

Make a well in the middle of the dry ingredients. Add wet ingredients and mix with as few strokes as possible. Don't overmix. Spoon batter into muffin tins. Bake at 350° for 25 minutes.

Yield: 10 muffins

Lemon Poppy Seed Muffins

⅜ cup butter or margarine (6 tablespoons)

¼ cup poppy seeds

½ cup lemon juice

3 large eggs, beaten

¾ cup buttermilk

zest and juice of 2 lemons

3 cups unbleached white flour

1 cup sugar

2 teaspoons baking powder

1 teaspoon baking soda

½ teaspoon salt

Preheat oven to 350°. Grease muffin tins. Melt butter or margarine and let cool. Soak the poppy seeds in lemon juice for 10 minutes while preparing the other ingredients.

Combine all the dry ingredients in a large bowl. In a medium-sized bowl, whisk together the melted butter or margarine, eggs, and buttermilk. Add the zest and juice of the lemons and the poppy seeds and juice they were soaking in and mix well.

Make a well in the middle of the dry ingredients. Add wet ingredients and mix with as few strokes as possible. Don't overmix. Spoon batter into muffin tins. Bake at 350° for 20 to 25 minutes.

Yield: 1 dozen muffins

Blueberry–Lemon–Honey Muffins

¼ cup butter or margarine

2 cups unbleached white flour
1 teaspoon baking powder
1 teaspoon baking soda
1 teaspoon salt

1 cup fresh or frozen blueberries

2 large eggs, beaten
½ cup honey
½ cup buttermilk
zest of 1 lemon

Preheat oven to 350°. Grease the muffin tins. Melt the butter or margarine and let cool.

In a medium-sized bowl, combine the dry ingredients. In a small bowl, coat the blueberries with 1 cup of the dry mix and add back to the dry mix. In another medium-sized bowl, whisk together the melted butter or margarine, eggs, honey, buttermilk, and zest.

Make a well in the middle of the dry ingredients. Add wet ingredients and mix with as few strokes as possible. Don't overmix. Spoon batter into muffin tins. Bake at 350° for 20 minutes.

Yield: 10 muffins

VARIATIONS

- For Blueberry Almond Muffins, omit the lemon zest and add ½ teaspoon almond extract to the wet mix.

- For Blueberry Cinnamon Muffins, omit the lemon zest and add 1 teaspoon cinnamon to the dry mix.

Ginger–Orange–Honey Muffins

¼ cup butter or margarine

2 cups unbleached white flour

1 teaspoon cinnamon

½ teaspoon nutmeg

½ teaspoon ground ginger

1 teaspoon baking soda

1 teaspoon baking powder

½ teaspoon salt

2 large eggs, beaten

½ cup molasses

¼ cup honey

½ cup buttermilk

1 teaspoon orange zest

2 teaspoons finely grated fresh
   ginger

Preheat oven to 350°. Grease muffin tins. Melt butter or margarine and let cool.

Mix all the dry ingredients in a medium-sized bowl. In another medium-sized bowl, whisk together all wet ingredients, including the butter or margarine, orange zest, and fresh ginger.

Make a well in the middle of the dry ingredients. Add wet ingredients and mix with as few strokes as possible. Don't overmix. Spoon batter into muffin tins. Bake at 350° for 20 minutes.

Yield: 10 muffins

Pumpkin–Orange–Honey Muffins

¼ cup butter or margarine

2 cups unbleached white flour
1 teaspoon baking soda
1 teaspoon baking powder
½ teaspoon salt

½ cup orange juice concentrate
2 large eggs, beaten
¾ cup canned pumpkin purée
½ cup sour cream
¾ cup honey
zest of 1 orange

Preheat oven to 350°. Grease muffin tins. Melt butter or margarine and let cool.

In a large bowl, mix all the dry ingredients. In a medium-sized bowl, mix the butter or margarine, orange juice concentrate, eggs, pumpkin purée, sour cream, honey, and orange zest until well blended.

Make a well in the middle of the dry ingredients. Add wet ingredients and mix with as few strokes as possible. Don't overmix. Spoon batter into muffin tins. Bake at 350° for 15 to 20 minutes, until muffins are golden brown on top.

Yield: 13 muffins (a baker's dozen)

COFFEE CAKES

We think of weekends as a time for gathering and celebration, a time for a little added touch from the kitchen. That's why we generally serve coffee cakes only on the weekends. Our pieces of coffee cake are often huge, and we like to stack them up high and put them on the counter in plain view of our weekend clientele.

Our typical coffee cake is made with a lightly sweetened batter or dough and filled with whatever fresh fruits or berries are in season—fresh blueberries picked at a local customer's blueberry patch, or fresh strawberries and raspberries from fruit farms on the island. Apples, peaches, and pears are all grown in our region, often organically. Sometimes when the harvests are especially plentiful, we freeze fruits and berries to use during the winter. When nothing else is available, we get fruit from the supply houses.

Some of our coffee cakes are made with yeasted doughs. If you are new to baking yeasted doughs, you might want to turn to page 81 for some practical tips to help get you started.

Blueberry Sour Cream Coffee Cake

This moist, buttery crumb cake rises high in our ovens. We substitute layers of other fruit in season such as peaches, raspberries, or strawberries. Our Poppy Seed Coffee Cake (see recipe below) is another delectable variation.

½ cup butter or margarine, room
    temperature
1 cup sugar
3 eggs
zest of 1 lemon

2 cups unbleached white flour
1 teaspoon baking powder
1 teaspoon baking soda
¼ teaspoon salt
1 cup sour cream

Crumb Topping (see page 222)
1 cup fresh or frozen blueberries

Preheat oven to 350° and grease an 8-inch square pan. Cream the butter with an electric mixer. Add the sugar and beat until light in color and fluffy. Beat in the eggs, one at a time. Add the lemon zest and beat again.

In a medium-sized bowl, mix together the flour, baking powder, baking soda, and salt. Add the flour to the creamed mixture alternately with the sour cream. Beat until the batter is smooth.

Prepare the Crumb Topping.

Pour half of the batter into the pan. Spread the blueberries evenly over the batter. Pour the remaining batter over the blueberries. Sprinkle the Crumb Topping evenly over the batter.

Bake at 350° for 1 hour and 10 minutes or until a toothpick inserted in the middle comes out clean.

Yield: One 8-inch square coffee cake

For Poppy Seed Coffee Cake, follow the directions for the Blueberry Sour Cream Coffee Cake, but omit the blueberries and substitute the following filling:

Poppy Seed Filling

$^1/_3$ *cup poppy seeds*
$^1/_2$ *cup milk*
$^1/_2$ *cup pine nuts, coarsely ground*
zest of 1 lemon
$^1/_4$ *cup sugar*
$^1/_4$ *teaspoon almond extract*

Combine the poppy seeds and milk in a small saucepan and simmer for 10 minutes, stirring occasionally. Add the pine nuts and lemon zest. Continue cooking for another few minutes. Add the sugar and cook for another few minutes until the mixture thickens. Remove from heat and add almond extract. Cool and use in place of the blueberries.

Pear Kuchen

In the autumn, when pears and plums are ripening, and our windows are steamy from all of the baking, we serve *kuchen*, a German-style fruit pie, at the Streamliner Diner. Our Pear Kuchen is a light, anise-flavored coffee cake. The delicate flavors and textures go well with a cup of tea.

½ cup butter, room temperature	3 Bartlett pears
½ cup sugar	1 teaspoon anise seed
3 eggs	2 tablespoons lemon juice
1 cup unbleached white flour	2 tablespoons sugar
½ teaspoon vanilla	
½ teaspoon anise extract	
2 tablespoons grated lemon zest	

Preheat oven to 350°. Grease a 12-inch round pizza pan. Cream the butter with an electric mixer. Add the sugar gradually and continue beating until light and fluffy. Add the eggs, one at a time, beating well after each addition. Add the flour, vanilla, anise extract, and lemon zest and mix thoroughly. Pour the batter into the pizza pan.

To make the pear topping, peel the pears, cut them in half, core, and stem. Maintaining the pear shape, slice each half in half again, from top to bottom. Now cut the curved piece from the outside edge of each pear in half lengthwise. Lay these pieces in a mosaic pattern over the batter, pressing them in slightly. Sprinkle the top with the anise seeds, lemon juice, and sugar.

Bake at 350° for 25 to 30 minutes until the kuchen is set in the middle and the outside edge is starting to brown.

Yield: One 12-inch round kuchen

VARIATIONS

For Plum Kuchen, omit the anise extract and seeds, lemon zest and juice, and pears. Substitute 2 pounds Italian prune plums cut in half and pitted. Layer the plums, overlapping on the batter, up to ½ inch from the edge. Press plums in slightly. Sprinkle with 3 tablespoons sugar and bake as directed above.

Lemon Cream Cheese Braid

1 tablespoon active dry yeast

½ cup unbleached white flour

½ cup warm water

¼ cup butter

¼ cup sugar

2 large eggs

2 teaspoons lemon zest

1 teaspoon salt

2 to 2¼ cups unbleached white
   flour

8 ounces cream cheese

½ cup sugar

zest and juice of 1 lemon

1 egg, beaten

In a small bowl, mix the yeast and ½ cup flour together with a wire whisk. Add the water and whisk thoroughly. Cover and let rise to double in size in a warm, draft-free place, approximately 10 minutes.

In a medium-sized bowl, cream the butter with an electric mixer. Add ¼ cup sugar and beat until the mixture is light yellow and fluffy. Add two eggs, beating them in one at a tme. Beat in the 2 teaspoons lemon zest. Using a rubber spatula or spoon, stir in the flour-yeast mixture and the salt. Begin adding the flour, stirring in about ½ cup at a time, until the dough is too stiff to stir.

Turn the dough out onto your work area and knead in the rest of the flour. The dough should be smooth and elastic, and a little on the wet side. It should grab the work surface and let go. Clean and oil the mixing bowl. Return the dough to the bowl, cover, and let rise to double in size, approximately 45 minutes.

To make the filling, beat the cream cheese and ½ cup sugar together in a small mixing bowl until light and fluffy in texture. Add the zest and juice of 1 lemon and beat it in thoroughly. Set aside until you are ready to put the braid together.

Roll the dough out to make a 12 × 14-inch rectangle about ½ inch thick.

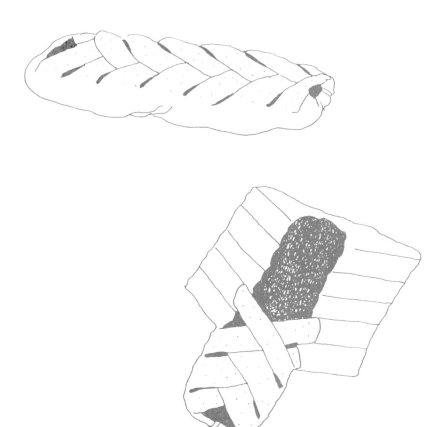

Fold the rectangle in half lengthwise. Cut diagonally along the lengthwise open edge, making 3-inch cuts toward the center fold, 1 inch apart. Unfold, so that the rectangle has strands fanning out on either side. Spoon the cream cheese filling down the middle of the dough and interlace the strands over the filling.

Grease an 11½ × 17½-inch baking sheet. Set the braid on the sheet and let rise again for 20 minutes.

Brush the top of the braid with the beaten egg. Bake in a preheated 350° oven for 25 to 30 minutes. Cool before serving.

Yield: 1 coffee cake

Cinnamon Rolls

Irene's cinnamon rolls are adapted from a recipe she found on the back of a yeast package thirty years ago. Our customers love to watch her roll out the dough on our huge marble countertop. She spreads on the cinnamon, sugar, and butter with a rubber spatula and rolls the dough into a long snake. These rolls are almost as easy to make as they are to eat.

½ cup milk	½ cup butter, melted
½ cup granulated sugar	1 cup brown sugar
1 teaspoon salt	1 tablespoon cinnamon
½ cup butter, softened	2 cups chopped walnuts or pecans
2 tablespoons active dry yeast	
½ cup warm water	4 tablespoons butter, softened
2 eggs, lightly beaten	1 cup powdered sugar, sifted
4½ to 5 cups unbleached white flour	1½ tablespoons lemon juice

In a small saucepan, scald the milk. Pour the hot milk over the granulated sugar, salt, and ½ cup butter. Cool to lukewarm. In a large bowl, dissolve the yeast in warm water. Let sit for 5 minutes until the yeast is bubbly. Add the lukewarm milk mixture to the dissolved yeast and stir. With a wire whisk, beat in the eggs. Add 1 cup of flour at a time, stirring until smooth. Add enough flour to make a soft dough. Turn out onto a lightly floured board or cloth. Knead, adding flour as needed, until the dough is smooth and elastic but not sticky. Place in a greased bowl, cover, and let rise until double in bulk, approximately 45 minutes. Punch down.

Grease two baking sheets. Roll the dough into a rectangle about 15 × 22 inches.

In a small bowl, mix together ½ cup melted butter and 1 cup brown sugar. Using a rubber spatula, spread this over the dough up to ½ inch from the edge of the pan. Sprinkle the cinnamon evenly over the sugar and butter. Top with a layer of nuts. Roll the dough up lengthwise, jelly-roll fashion, to make a log and pinch the edge to seal. Slice into 14 pieces. Place 1 inch apart on baking sheets and let rise for 15 minutes.

Preheat oven to 350°. Bake rolls for 30 minutes or until lightly browned on top.

To prepare the glaze, beat 4 tablespoons of butter with powdered sugar and lemon juice. Brush the glaze on top of the warm rolls after baking. These rolls are delicious served warm or cold.

Yield: 14 rolls

Kolaches

This recipe was passed down by Alexandra's grandmother, Lydia Blazek Calvin, and is printed in memory of her. Alexandra remembers, with great fondness, the days she spent on her grandparents' farm in central Texas. Her grandma would be up before the crack of dawn baking biscuits, frying chunks of home-cured bacon and fresh eggs, and percolating thick black coffee while her grand-daddy was out milking the cows. They'd have everything done by the time they roused the grandkids from their sleep and the sun would just be rising over the mesquite trees. The smell of those biscuits wafting through the rooms left a distinct path by which the sleepy children made their way to the breakfast table. For a special treat Grandma sometimes made traditional Czech pastries called *kolaches*. Everyone loved these fruit- or cheese-filled sweets. Try your own fillings using fresh apricots, berries, or apples, or use fruit preserves.

¼ cup warm water
1 tablespoon sugar
2 teaspoons active dry yeast

1 cup milk
½ cup sugar
1 teaspoon salt
½ cup butter or margarine, softened
2 eggs, beaten
4½ to 5 cups unbleached white flour

1 recipe of filling (see following pages)

2 tablespoons sugar
2 tablespoons flour
1 tablespoon butter

Mix the warm water and 1 tablespoon sugar in a large bowl. Sprinkle in the yeast, stirring until dissolved. Let stand for 5 minutes or until the mixture bubbles.

Scald the milk in a small saucepan. With a wire whisk, stir the ½ cup sugar, salt, and ½ cup butter or margarine into the scalded milk. Cool to warm temperature, then stir in the eggs. Stir the lukewarm milk into the yeast mixture and beat until smooth. Stir in the flour a cup at a time until it is fully incorporated and no longer sticky. Turn the dough onto a floured surface and knead for about 5 minutes or until the dough does not stick to the hands. Put the dough into a greased bowl, cover with a damp towel, and let rise in a warm place for 1 hour or until double in bulk.

Prepare the filling (see recipes below).

Turn the dough out onto a lightly floured surface. Divide it into 12 equal pieces and form each into a ball by hand. Press very hard with a tablespoon to make a crater in the top of each mound, using fingers if necessary to help form the indentation. Spoon the filling of your choice into the indentation in the top of each kolache. Each one holds about 1 heaping tablespoon of filling.

To make the crumb topping, mix together 2 tablespoons sugar and 2 tablespoons flour. Using your fingers, rub in 1 tablespoon butter until fully incorporated. The mixture should be crumbly. Sprinkle crumb topping on the filling.

Place kolaches 1 inch apart on greased cookie sheets. Bake at 350° for 20 minutes.

Yield: 1 dozen kolaches

Poppy Seed Filling

4 *tablespoons butter*
8 *tablespoons poppy seeds*
4 *tablespoons sugar*

Melt butter in a small saucepan. Soak poppy seeds in the butter for 10 minutes. Add sugar and stir.

Cottage Cheese Filling

$^{1}/_{2}$ cup cottage cheese
2 tablespoons sugar
1 egg, beaten

Combine all the ingredients.

Fresh Peach Filling

1 tablespoon butter
2 peaches, diced
2 tablespoons sugar

Melt butter in a small saucepan. Add peaches and sugar and cook over low heat for 10 minutes, stirring occasionally.

Prune Filling

1 cup pitted prunes
$^{1}/_{2}$ cup water

In a small saucepan, simmer prunes in water for 10 minutes until prunes have absorbed the water. Mash with a fork.

Cardamom–Ginger–Fig Pudding

Ever since D. H. Lawrence praised the fig for its sensuous properties, figs have been as closely associated with the advent of spring as are the greening of the earth and the fragrant unfolding of flower buds. We offer our baked fig pudding, with hints of cardamom, ginger, and brandy as a celebration of springtime.

2 cups dried figs	¼ cup orange juice
1 tablespoon minced lemon zest	¼ cup brandy
1 cup orange juice	1 cup brown sugar
½ cup butter, softened	½ cup butter
1 cup granulated sugar	¼ teaspoon cardamom
2 eggs	

2 cups unbleached white flour
1 teaspoon baking soda
1 teaspoon baking powder
1 teaspoon cardamom
1 teaspoon ground ginger
1 cup finely chopped walnuts
¾ cup buttermilk

Preheat oven to 350°. Grease a 10-inch tube or bundt pan.

In a small saucepan, simmer the figs and lemon zest in 1 cup orange juice for 10 minutes. Purée in a blender or food processor. Set aside.

In a large bowl, cream ½ cup butter with an electric mixer until light and fluffy. Slowly add the granulated sugar while continuing to cream until the mixture is light yellow in color. Add the eggs, one at a time, beating after each addition. Beat in the fig mixture.

In a medium-sized bowl, sift together the flour, baking soda, baking powder, 1 teaspoon cardamom, and ginger. Stir in the walnuts. Using a rubber spatula, fold the buttermilk and the flour alternately into the fig mixture, a little at a time, until all of the ingredients are incorporated.

Pour the batter into the tube or bundt pan and bake at 350° for 1 hour, or until a knife inserted in the middle comes out clean. Remove from the oven and set aside to cool while preparing the sauce.

To make the sauce, combine ¼ cup orange juice, brandy, brown sugar, ½ cup butter, and ¼ teaspoon cardamom in a small saucepan. Cook over a low heat for 15 minutes or longer to create a fairly thick syrup, stirring frequently.

Remove the pudding from the pan and pour the warm sauce over the whole pudding or over individual servings. Serve warm.

Yield: One 10-inch tube or bundt cake

Cinnamon Sticks: Two Traditions

Liz's grandmothers were not adventuresome cooks. One grandmother, Adelaide Hickox (a.k.a. "Hiccups"), couldn't even boil water, according to Liz's Uncle Sumner. Her other grandmother, Florence Chapman (a.k.a. "Gabby"), loved sweets, and for her, afternoon teatime was a family ritual. She was not a great baker, though, and whenever Liz's family visited, she'd have on hand a box of cookies or pastries from the bakery. At Eastertime, it was freshly baked sweet buns from the hot-cross-bun man. On special occasions, there was one thing she did make to serve with tea—Cinnamon Sticks. Gabby would buy a loaf of freshly baked white bread, cut it into rectangles an inch thick and three inches long, and roll these in melted butter and cinnamon sugar. She'd bake them in a hot oven until bubbly and crisp and serve them hot out of the oven. They never had a chance to cool down, as they quickly disappeared.

Here's another cinnamon stick story—this one about Irene's Oma Lisa, who used to roll out leftover pie dough scraps, cut them into strips, sprinkle them with cinnamon sugar, twist, and bake them until crispy. These treats were handed to the hungry, pestering grandchildren.

BRUNCH

On Saturdays and Sundays, the lines out the door reflect the popularity of our breakfasts and brunches. On weekends, many Seattle-ites take the ferry to Bainbridge Island and walk the ten minutes to our restaurant. Hungry bicyclists stop by on their tour of the island. From the moment the door opens, customers fill the thirty-four seats in the diner.

Our brunches usually have eggs hidden in them somewhere, whether poached on top of something, as in our English Muffin Specials and Huevos Rancheros, or baked in a custard, as in Julie's Croustade French Toast. We have customers who telephone to ask when we'll be serving their favorite brunch. That's a hard question to answer since we sometimes go for months without repeating a brunch special. In this section we present recipes for many of those most-requested weekend specials so you can try them out in your own kitchens.

Brunch and breakfast is all we serve on weekends. Because we are so busy and speed is essential, we focus on dishes that are easy to serve. The preparation of the brunch is usually a big job, but most of the work is done the day before serving. All we have to do in the morning is assemble and heat.

Julie's Croustade French Toast

Croissants baked in a vanilla-cinnamon custard and glazed with a cinnamon-orange butter—it's a dish that will melt in your mouth. This easy-to-make dish was invented by Julie, one of our fine chefs.

4 croissants	½ cup butter
6 eggs	3 tablespoons honey
2 cups half-and-half	½ teaspoon cinnamon
⅓ cup whipping cream	1 tablespoon orange zest, grated
1 teaspoon vanilla	
½ cup sugar	
½ teaspoon cinnamon	

Preheat oven to 350°. Grease a 9×9-inch baking pan. Cut each croissant into four chunks. Line the baking pan with the croissants, with the crust facing up.

In a medium-sized bowl, beat the eggs with a wire whisk. Whisk in the half-and-half, whipping cream, and vanilla. In a small bowl, combine the sugar and ½ teaspoon of cinnamon. Whisk this into the egg batter. Pour the batter over the croissants and allow the croissants to soak for 10 minutes. Turn them over just before baking.

Bake at 350° for 45 minutes or until the custard is set. Cover with foil if the croustade is getting too dark.

While the croustade is baking, cream the butter in the small bowl of an electric mixer until light and fluffy. Beat in the honey, ½ teaspoon cinnamon, and orange zest.

To serve, cut the croustade into squares. Serve hot, topping each serving with a little cinnamon-orange butter.

Yield: 4 to 6 servings

Peasant Brunch Squares

This brunch dish is an all-in-one meal in a potato crust. It might appear time-consuming to make, but the potato shell can be prepared and stuffed ahead of time. About 1½ hours before you are ready to serve, add the beaten eggs and bake. This dish is delicious with other fillings such as fish or poultry.

6 potatoes, diced (8 cups)

½ cup butter or margarine

1 onion, diced

4 cloves garlic, minced

1 teaspoon salt

1 teaspoon pepper

1 teaspoon caraway seeds

1 tablespoon butter or margarine

1 green pepper, diced

1 pound ham, diced

2 tablespoons fresh oregano, chopped

¼ cup minced parsley

8 eggs

2¼ cups milk

1 teaspoon salt

½ teaspoon pepper

Preheat oven to 375°. Grease a 9 × 13-inch baking pan. Steam the potatoes until they are just tender, approximately 10 minutes. Put them in a large bowl and set them aside.

In a skillet, heat the butter or margarine until bubbly. Add the onion and sauté until the onion becomes transparent. Add garlic and cook 2 more minutes. Add to the potatoes. Stir in 1 teaspoon salt, 1 teaspoon pepper, and caraway seeds. Press the potatoes into the baking pan, building up the sides like a pie shell. Bake at 375° for 30 minutes, until lightly browned.

Meanwhile heat 1 tablespoon butter or margarine in a large skillet. Sauté the green pepper until limp. Add the ham, oregano, and parsley. Cook 2 more minutes. Fill the baked potato shell with this mixture. The dish can be cooled and refrigerated at this point if you are preparing it ahead of time.

Beat the eggs with a wire whisk. Add the milk, 1 teaspoon salt, and

½ teaspoon pepper and whisk. Pour this over the vegetable and ham mixture. Bake at 350° for 40 minutes, or until the eggs have set. The baking time will lengthen if the crust has been refrigerated. Remove and cool slightly before serving.

Yield: 6 servings

Fruit Kugel

Kugel is a German word meaning something round. In cooking, it refers to a casserole-type dish baked in a round container. Our Fruit Kugel features nectarines and apples in an egg-and-cheese custard, finished off with a raspberry sauce. It's a light dish, ideal for breakfast. If you read the ingredients (noodles for breakfast!) you'll probably scrunch up your nose and turn to a more conventional recipe. Trust us! Fruit Kugel is unbelievably delicious. We bake it in a square pan, but if you want to be traditional, you can bake it in a round one.

6 ounces wide egg noodles	2 slices whole wheat bread
2 tablespoons butter, melted	2 tablespoons butter, melted
2 eggs, slightly beaten	2 cups fresh raspberries (or 12
½ cup honey	ounces frozen)
1½ cups ricotta cheese	1¼ cups apple juice
½ teaspoon vanilla	2 tablespoons tapioca
1 apple, grated	2 tablespoons honey
zest of 1 lemon, grated	
juice of 1 lemon	
1 nectarine, diced	
½ cup raisins	
⅔ teaspoon salt	
1 teaspoon cinnamon	

Cook the noodles and drain them. Return them to the pot and toss with 2 tablespoons of butter. Preheat oven to 350°. Grease a 9 × 9-inch baking pan.

In a large bowl, combine the eggs, ½ cup honey, ricotta, and vanilla. Add the apple, lemon zest and juice, nectarine, raisins, salt, and cinnamon and mix well. Toss with the buttered noodles until mixed thoroughly. Pour into the greased pan.

In a blender or food processer make crumbs of the bread. Add 2 tablespoons of melted butter and process briefly. Spread the crumbs evenly over the kugel. Bake at 350° for 30 minutes.

To prepare the raspberry sauce, combine the raspberries, apple juice, and tapioca in a small saucepan. Set aside for 15 minutes to dissolve the tapioca. Cook over medium heat, stirring constantly. When the mixture begins to simmer, lower the heat and continue cooking for 10 minutes. Remove from heat and sweeten with 2 tablespoons honey. Serve warm over the hot kugel.

Yield: 4 to 6 servings

Our customers have always enjoyed our selection of omelettes. We have eight different combinations on our menu: Denver, Cheddar, Tomato–Bacon–Avocado, Spinach–Mushroom–Green Onion, Greek, Cajun, Mexican, and Tomato–Bacon–Blue Cheese. Each is served with a hot muffin and fresh fruit. Here are three of our favorites, beginning with the Mexican Omelette, which is undoubtedly the most popular of them all.

Mexican Omelette

2 *potatoes, diced*

4 *tablespoons vegetable oil or butter*

1 *4-ounce can chopped green chilies*

1 *cup chopped green onions*

4 *tablespoons vegetable oil or butter*

12 *eggs*

2 *cups grated cheddar cheese*

1 *cup Streamliner Salsa (see page 230)*

1 *cup Guacamole (see page 232)*

In a steamer pot, or in a small saucepan with a small amount of boiling water, steam the diced potatoes for 10 minutes, until just tender. Remove from heat and drain. Heat 4 tablespoons of oil or butter in a medium-sized frying pan. Sauté the green chilies and green onions in the oil or butter, stirring frequently, for 3 minutes. Add the potatoes and turn heat to low.

For each omelette, heat 1 tablespoon oil or butter in an omelette pan over medium heat. Pour 3 beaten eggs into the hot pan, and swirl it around so that the eggs cover the bottom of the pan. When the eggs have set up sufficiently to get a spatula underneath, flip the omelette.

Cover one half of each omelette with ½ cup grated cheese and ¼ of the vegetable mixture. Fold over the omelette to make the familiar half-moon shape and cover the pan so that the cheese melts. When all four are ready, serve immediately. (You can make several omelettes at once, if you have the pans.) Top each with ¼ cup salsa and ¼ cup guacamole.

Yield: 4 servings

Tomato–Bacon–Avocado Omelette

2 tablespoons vegetable oil or
  butter
8 thick slices bacon, cooked and
  diced
1 cup tomatoes, diced

4 tablespoons vegetable oil or
  butter
12 eggs
1 avocado, sliced
2 cups grated cheddar cheese
½ cup sour cream
4 sprigs parsley, washed

Heat the oil or butter in a medium-sized frying pan. Sauté the diced bacon and tomatoes in the oil or butter over medium heat for 1 minute

Prepare omelettes as for Mexican Omelette, using 1 tablespoon oil or butter and 3 eggs for each omelette. Fill each omelette with bacon and tomatoes, avocado slices, and ½ cup cheddar cheese. Fold and cover so that the cheese melts. Before serving, garnish each omelette with a heaping tablespoon of sour cream and a parsley sprig.

Yield: 4 servings

Spinach–Mushroom–Green Onion Omelette

1 bunch spinach leaves
2 tablespoons oil or butter
1 cup sliced mushrooms
1 cup finely chopped green onions

4 tablespoons vegetable oil or
  butter
12 eggs
2 cups grated cheddar cheese
½ cup sour cream
4 sprigs parsley, washed

Wash and drain the spinach. Heat the oil or butter in a medium-sized frying pan. Sauté the mushrooms and green onions in the oil or butter, stirring frequently, for 3 minutes. Add the spinach, cover, lower heat, and cook for 1 minute.

Prepare the omelettes as for Mexican Omelettes, using 1 tablespoon oil or butter and 3 eggs for each omelette. Fill each omelette with spinach-mushroom mixture and ½ cup cheddar cheese. Fold and cover the pan so that the cheese melts. Before serving, garnish each omelette with a heaping tablespoon of sour cream and a parsley sprig.

Yield: 4 servings

Streamliner Huevos Rancheros

This dish is our variation on the classic Mexican breakfast. We serve two poached eggs on a bed of our refried beans, topped with our own salsa and melted cheddar cheese. A handful of corn tortilla chips accompanies this popular dish. If you have the beans and salsa all ready, this is a cinch to make.

    8 eggs
    3 cups Refried Beans (see
       page 231)
    2 cups Streamliner Salsa (see
       page 230)
    1 cup grated cheddar cheese
    3 cups tortilla chips

Preheat oven to 400°. Poach the eggs. For each serving, spoon ¾ cup beans onto a dish. Top with two poached eggs, ½ cup salsa, and ¼ cup cheese. Bake for 5 minutes or until the cheese has melted. Serve piping hot with a handful of tortilla chips on the side.

Yield: 4 servings

Breakfast Burritos

Our Breakfast Burritos consist of two scrambled eggs and refried beans wrapped in a soft flour tortilla, topped with fresh salsa, sour cream, and black olives. They are a popular and filling breakfast. For lunch we substitute cheddar cheese for the eggs—about ⅓ cup grated cheese for each burrito.

> 3 cups Refried Beans (see
>   page 231)
> 8 eggs
> 4 teaspoons butter or margarine
> 4 flour tortillas
> 1 cup Streamliner Salsa (see
>   page 230)
> ½ cup sour cream
> ½ cup sliced black olives

Reheat beans in a skillet, if necessary.

To scramble the eggs, beat the eggs until foamy in a large bowl using a wire whisk. In a large frying pan over medium heat, heat the butter or margarine until it bubbles. Whisking the eggs, pour them into the hot pan. With a spatula, stir and flip the eggs constantly until they are soft or well scrambled, depending on how you like them.

To soften the tortillas, heat them in a frying pan over medium heat, a few seconds on each side. Fill each tortilla with ¾ cup beans and 2 scrambled eggs. Roll up and top each burrito with ¼ cup salsa, 2 tablespoons sour cream, and 2 tablespoons black olives.

Yield: 4 servings

Borderline Brunch

We serve this as a platter on weekend mornings—Mexican-style rice with hot corn tortillas, scrambled eggs, fresh homemade salsa, and guacamole—for a satisfying Tex-Mex brunch.

1 recipe White Rice (see page 226)

1 onion, chopped
¼ cup olive oil
3 cloves garlic, minced
2 jalapeño peppers, seeded and minced
1 tablespoon coriander seeds, crushed
2 tablespoons boiling water
zest of 1 lemon
¼ cup chopped cilantro leaves
1 teaspoon salt

12 eggs
2 to 4 tablespoons butter or margarine
12 corn tortillas

Streamliner Salsa (see page 230)
Guacamole (see page 232)

Prepare the rice and keep covered until ready to mix.

In a small skillet, sauté the onion in the oil until the onion is transparent. Add the garlic and peppers and sauté for 2 more minutes. Remove from heat.

In a small saucepan, steep the coriander seeds in 2 tablespoons boiling water for a few minutes, strain, and add the liquid to the onion mixture along with the lemon zest, cilantro leaves, and salt. Mix the onion mixture with the rice, being careful not to compress the rice.

Beat the eggs until foamy, using a wire whisk. In a large frying pan over medium heat, heat 2 to 4 tablespoons of butter or margarine until it bubbles. Whisking the eggs, pour them into the hot pan. Stir and flip the eggs with a spatula until they are soft or well scrambled, depending on how you like them. Remove from heat and cover until ready to serve.

To soften the tortillas, heat them in a frying pan over medium heat, a few seconds each side. On each platter arrange two corn tortillas, scrambled eggs, and the Mexican-style rice topped with salsa and guacamole. Serve immediately.

Yield: 6 servings

One of our basic brunch themes is our English Muffin Specials. These are an elaboration of the classic Eggs Benedict. The base of the English Muffin Special is, of course, a toasted English muffin. It's topped with two poached eggs and smothered with a delicious sauce of your choice. Like omelettes, the muffin platters can be varied in endless ways. We have included several of our favorite combinations.

Streamliner Rarebit

4 tablespoons butter

4 tablespoons flour

4 cups milk

½ cup grated Parmesan cheese

½ cup grated sharp cheddar or
   Swiss cheese

2 tablespoons Dijon mustard

1 teaspoon Worcestershire sauce

pinch of cayenne pepper
   (optional)

1 teaspoon prepared horseradish

1 teaspoon salt

¼ teaspoon black pepper

6 English muffins

12 eggs

12 slices tomato

18 slices bacon, cooked

In a 2-quart saucepan, heat the butter over medium heat until bubbly. Add the flour and stir to make a smooth paste. Continue to cook, stirring continuously, until the flour starts to turn golden. Add the milk, whisking briskly to avoid lumps. Lower heat. Stir the sauce occasionally to avoid scorching, and cook it until it begins to thicken. Add the grated cheeses, Dijon mustard, Worcestershire, optional cayenne pepper, horseradish, salt, and pepper. Stir until the cheeses melt.

Preheat oven to 300°. Toast the English muffins, and place them in the oven to keep warm. Poach the eggs.

Layer the following on each half of an English muffin: a tomato slice, poached egg, bacon, and sauce. Serve immediately.

Yield: 6 servings

Mediterranean Sunrise

Colorful as a sunrise, this English Muffin Special combines the Mediterranean flavors of artichoke hearts, fresh basil, capers, and wine served over poached eggs on an English muffin.

2 8½-ounce cans artichoke hearts packed in water	1½ teaspoons salt
	¼ teaspoon pepper
4 tablespoons butter	1 cup minced parsley
3 tablespoons olive oil	3 tablespoons capers
2 cloves garlic, minced	½ cup white wine
1 onion, diced	
	6 English muffins
2 cups sliced mushrooms	12 eggs
2 cups diced Roma tomatoes	6 sprigs parsley
½ cup chopped fresh basil leaves (1 ounce)	2 lemons, cut in wedges

Drain and slice the artichoke hearts and set aside. Heat the butter and oil in a 3-quart soup pot on high heat. Sauté the garlic and onion until the onion becomes transparent. Add the mushrooms, artichoke hearts, and tomatoes, one ingredient at a time, cooking each new addition for 2 minutes before adding the next. Add the basil, salt, pepper, minced parsley, capers, and white wine. Simmer for 10 to 15 minutes on low heat. Turn off.

Preheat oven to 300°. Toast the English muffins and pop them in the oven. Poach the eggs. For each serving, put two English muffin halves on the plate, and top each half with a poached egg and plenty of sauce. Garnish with a sprig of parsley and lemon wedges.

Note: You can also serve this over rice in the evening for a Mediterranean Sunset!

Yield: 6 servings

Basil Cream English Muffins

3 whole cloves

1 onion

4 tablespoons butter

3 tablespoons flour

4 cups milk, heated

1 bay leaf

1½ cups fresh basil leaves (3 ounces)

1 clove garlic, minced

½ cup grated Parmesan cheese

1 teaspoon salt

½ teaspoon pepper

4 English muffins

8 eggs

8 slices tomato

12 slices bacon, cooked

¼ cup grated Parmesan cheese

Stick the cloves in the onion, sputnik-like, and set aside. In a 2-quart saucepan, heat butter until bubbly. Add the flour and stir to make a smooth paste. Continue to cook, stirring continuously, until the flour starts to turn golden. Add the milk, whisking briskly to avoid lumps. Lower heat. Stir sauce occasionally to avoid scorching. Add the onion and bay leaf, and continue cooking on low heat for 20 minutes. Remove the onion and bay leaf.

Purée the basil leaves in a blender or food processor and add to the sauce along with the garlic. Stir to incorporate. Add ½ cup Parmesan cheese, salt, and pepper, stirring to melt the cheese. Remove sauce from heat and cover to keep hot.

Preheat oven to 300°. Toast the English muffins and place them in the oven to keep warm. Poach the eggs. Layer the following on each half of English muffin: tomato slice, poached egg, basil cream sauce, and bacon. Sprinkle the remaining ¼ cup Parmesan cheese on top and serve immediately.

Yield: 4 servings

Lemon Chicken English Muffins

1⅓ pounds chicken pieces

4 cups water

1 onion

1 carrot

1 stalk celery

3 sprigs parsley

2 cloves garlic

1 teaspoon dried dill weed

1 teaspoon salt

¼ teaspoon pepper

4 tablespoons butter

3 tablespoons flour

2 egg yolks, beaten

zest and juice of 1 lemon

salt and pepper to taste

1 pound asparagus

5 English muffins

10 eggs

To prepare the chicken stock, bring chicken and water to a boil in a 3-quart saucepan or soup pot. Skim off scum until the broth is clear and add the onion, carrot, celery, parsley, garlic, dill weed, salt, and pepper. Reduce heat and simmer for 30 minutes or until the chicken is tender. Strain the broth and reserve. Bone and cube the chicken and grate the carrot. Set aside.

In a 2-quart saucepan, heat the butter over medium heat until bubbly. Add the flour and stir to make a smooth paste. Continue to cook, stirring continuously, until the flour starts to turn golden. Add the hot broth, stirring briskly to avoid lumps. Cook for approximately 10 minutes. Add a little of the sauce to the yolks, mix, then add back to the sauce. Stir to combine. Cook for another 2 minutes. Add the lemon zest and juice. Remove from heat, and add the chicken and carrot. Add salt and pepper to taste. Cover to keep hot.

In a vegetable steamer, steam the asparagus 3 to 5 minutes, until just tender.

Preheat oven to 300°. Toast the English muffins, and place them in the oven to keep warm. Poach the eggs. Layer the following on each half of English muffin: a poached egg, sauce, and asparagus.

Yield: 5 servings

The classic treatment for a blintz is to fill a crêpe with a sweetened cheese filling, fold it up, and fry it in a little butter. Top it with a fruit sauce and a sprinkle of cinnamon sugar and you can be sure of never having leftovers.

Crêpes are easy to make, and you can make them ahead of time and store them in the refrigerator for a few days, all stacked up and ready to make blintzes—or maybe some other dish. With crêpes, you can stretch your imagination. Fill them with the leftovers of last night's dinner, or with some stir-fried vegetables or sliced fruit. Irene's daughter even made an incredible layered cake using crêpes, vanilla pudding, chocolate sauce, and whipped cream.

This crêpe recipe comes from Mollie Katzen's *The Enchanted Broccoli Forest*; however, our method of making them is slightly different. Thanks to Mollie for giving us permission to use her recipe.

Crêpes

3 eggs, beaten
1⅓ cups milk
2 tablespoons butter, melted
¾ cup unbleached white flour
½ teaspoon salt
butter for frying

In a medium-sized bowl, mix together the eggs, milk, and melted butter. Briskly whisk in the flour and salt. Mix until the consistency is like thick cream. This mixture can also be processed in a blender. Cover and refrigerate for at least 1 hour.

Use a 10-inch crêpe or omelette pan with slanted sides. Heat the pan over medium heat. Brush with butter and wipe out the excess. Fill a ¼-cup measure with batter and pour the batter into the pan while tilting it to spread the batter evenly over the bottom. Let cook until the edges of the crêpe pull away from the sides and the surface no longer appears wet. Flip and cook the crêpe another few seconds on the other side. Remove it from the pan. Stack the crêpes on a plate until all the batter has been used up. At this point, either cover with plastic wrap and refrigerate until needed, or use immediately.

Yield: Ten 8-inch crêpes

Ricotta Cheese Blintzes

3 cups ricotta cheese

$1/4$ cup honey

$1/2$ cup raisins

dash of cinnamon

zest of 1 lemon, grated

juice of 1 lemon

pinch of salt

10 crêpes (see recipe above)

butter for frying

$1/4$ cup sugar

2 teaspoons cinnamon

In a medium-sized bowl, thoroughly mix together the ricotta cheese, honey, raisins, cinnamon, lemon zest and juice, and salt, using a large spoon. Divide the filling equally among the 10 crêpes, a generous $1/4$ cup per crêpe, spooning it into the center of each. To form the blintz, fold two sides of the crêpe in over the filling, then fold in the other two sides.

Fry the blintzes in a little butter until warm and golden brown on both sides. Mix together sugar and cinnamon and sprinkle it on top of the blintzes, or serve with Blueberry Syrup (recipe follows).

Yield: 10 blintzes

Blueberry Syrup

2 cups blueberries
½ cup apple juice
zest of 1 lemon, grated
juice of 1 lemon

¼ cup sugar
1 tablespoon cornstarch
¼ cup cold water

In a small saucepan, bring the berries, apple juice, and lemon zest to a boil. Add the lemon juice and sugar. Remove from heat. In a small bowl, dissolve the cornstarch in water. Add it to the blueberries and stir. Cook over low heat for 4 minutes until slightly thick and the cornstarch clears. Serve warm or refrigerate until needed.

Yield: 2 cups

Sweet Squash Blintzes

2½ pounds butternut or other
   sweet squash (3 cups cooked
   and mashed)
3 ounces cream cheese
¼ cup honey
½ teaspoon salt
1 teaspoon cinnamon
¼ teaspoon nutmeg
zest of 1 orange, grated
¼ cup raisins (optional)
10 crêpes (see page 66)

butter for frying
¾ cup sour cream
1 cup chopped almonds, toasted

Bake the whole squash at 350° until tender, about 1½ hours. When tender, remove the skin and seeds. Mash the pulp and add the cream cheese, honey, salt, cinnamon, nutmeg, orange zest, and optional raisins. Mix well. Divide the filling equally among the crêpes, spooning it into the center of each one. Fold two sides in over the filling, then fold in the other two sides.

Fry the blintzes in a little butter until golden brown on both sides. Serve topped with a dollop of sour cream and sprinkled with almonds.

Yield: 10 blintzes

Hangtown Fry

Legend has it that Hangtown Fry was invented in a prison in Nevada before the days of the automobile, when travel was slow. It's said that a prisoner on death row used his wits to prolong his miserable life by ordering foods for his final meal that were hard to come by or out of season. He asked for bacon and eggs with oysters from the Pacific coast and fresh mushrooms, which were very hard to find. If you're an oyster lover, try this dish. You don't need to go to jail first.

> 1 quart raw oysters
> 1 pound thick-sliced bacon
> 2 cups sliced mushrooms,
>   domestic or edible wild
>   varieties such as meadow
>   mushrooms or chanterelles
> 12 eggs, beaten

Drain and pick over the oysters for bits of shell. In a 2-quart saucepan, drop the oysters into boiling water to cover. Return to a boil and cook the oysters until they plump up and their edges begin to curl, about 1 to 2 minutes. Drain immediately and set the oysters aside.

Cut the bacon into 2-inch pieces and fry in a large frying pan until limp and slightly brown. Remove the bacon and pour off all but 2 tablespoons of the bacon fat. Fry the mushrooms in the bacon fat until limp and starting to brown. Return the oysters and bacon to the frying pan. Add the beaten eggs and stir until the eggs are set and scrambled. Serve immediately with English muffins, toast, or a side of home fries.

Yield: 6 servings

Potatoes Deluxe

A customer of ours claims that of all the breakfast foods she has sampled worldwide, our Potatoes Deluxe is her favorite. Served alone, it is a hearty dish; accompanied with poached eggs and a side of fresh salsa it becomes a grand meal. We top our Deluxes with either melted cheddar cheese, guacamole, or a combination of both.

2 potatoes, diced
1 onion, diced
1/4 teaspoon salt
pinch pepper
pinch paprika
3 tablespoons oil, butter, or
  margarine
4 green onions, finely chopped
4 mushrooms, thinly sliced

1 tomato, diced
1/2 bunch spinach leaves, washed
  and drained
1 cup grated cheddar cheese
1/4 to 1/2 cup Guacamole (see
  page 232)

Steam the potatoes until just tender, approximately 10 minutes. Mix the steamed potatoes with the onion, salt, pepper, and paprika. In a large frying pan, heat 2 tablespoons oil, butter, or margarine until bubbly. Add the potatoes and fry them over a high heat until golden brown, flipping frequently, for approximately 5 minutes. Turn heat to low and cover to keep hot.

In a small frying pan, heat the remaining 1 tablespoon oil, butter, or margarine until bubbly. Add the green onions and mushrooms and sauté until tender, approximately 3 minutes, stirring frequently. Add these vegetables to the pan with the potatoes. Mix well with the spatula.

Top the potato mixture with the tomatoes, spinach, and cheddar cheese. Cover, and cook on low heat for 3 to 5 minutes until the spinach has wilted and the cheese melts. To serve, top each portion with a heaping tablespoon of guacamole.

Yield: 2 to 4 servings

Chorizo–Polenta–Cheese Bake

For a spicy beginning to your day, try this delicious baked polenta dish. It's great for breakfast, lunch, or dinner. The chorizo needs to be made at least 4 hours before the dish is assembled, so you might want to do that the night before. You can also assemble the whole dish ahead of time and heat it before serving.

½ pound lean ground pork
½ teaspoon salt
1 tablespoon chili powder
1 clove garlic, minced
1 teaspoon oregano
1 tablespoon vinegar

1 recipe Polenta (see page 227)
1 tablespoon olive oil
½ green pepper, diced
1 onion, diced
2 cloves garlic, minced
¼ cup raisins
½ cup sliced black olives
5 bay leaves
½ teaspoon oregano
¼ cup Streamliner Salsa (see page 230)
2 cups grated cheddar cheese

For the chorizo, mix together the pork, salt, chili powder, garlic, oregano, and vinegar in a large bowl. Cover and chill in the refrigerator for at least 4 hours. This can be done the night before.

Prepare the polenta and set aside. Fry the chorizo in a large skillet until the meat loses its pink color. Drain off any fat and set the meat aside.

For the filling, heat the oil in a large skillet and sauté the green pepper and onion until the onion becomes transparent. Add the garlic, raisins, olives, bay leaves, oregano, and salsa. Cover and simmer over low heat for 25 minutes. Remove from heat. Remove the bay leaves. Add the chorizo and mix well.

Preheat oven to 350°. Grease an 8×8-inch baking pan. Spoon half of the polenta into the pan. Top with the chorizo and vegetables and 1 cup of cheddar cheese. Smooth the remaining polenta over the filling and top with remaining cheese. Cover with a lid or with foil and bake at 350° for 30 minutes. Uncover and bake 15 more minutes. Serve hot.

Yield: 4 servings

Spicy Sausage Scrapple

Scrapple is Pennsylvania Dutch in origin, an invention of the thrifty farmers who wanted to use every last bit of the pigs at slaughtering time. We mix sausage, fresh herbs, sautéed onions, and green peppers with polenta, our substitute for grits. Formed into a loaf, sliced, fried to a crisp golden brown, and served with two eggs any style, Spicy Sausage Scrapple has those certain satisfying flavors reminiscent of breakfast on the farm.

> 1 recipe Polenta (see page 227)
> ½ pound spicy Italian sausage
> 1 onion, diced
> 1 green pepper, diced
> 2 tablespoons butter or olive oil
> ½ cup minced parsley
> 1 teaspoon oregano
> ¼ cup chopped chives
> 1 teaspoon marjoram
> pinch of thyme
> 2 to 4 tablespoons butter or
>   margarine

Prepare the polenta. Set aside.

In a large frying pan, brown the sausage. Drain the grease and crumble the sausage into a large bowl. In the same pan, sauté the onion and green pepper in 2 tablespoons butter or oil until the onion becomes transparent. Stir in the parsley, oregano, chives, marjoram, and thyme. Combine this with the sausage. While the polenta is still hot, add it to the sausage-vegetable mixture and mix thoroughly. Spoon into a greased 5 × 9-inch bread pan. Press down to make an even loaf. Let cool.

Slice the loaf into 6 pieces. Heat 2 to 4 tablespoons butter in a large frying pan, and fry the scrapple over a medium-high heat until crispy brown on both sides.

Serve with 2 eggs, any style, and a fresh fruit cup, toast, or a fresh, hot muffin.

Note: You can make scrapple a day early by refrigerating it in the loaf pan. To keep it even longer, take it out of the pan and wrap it in plastic wrap. Fry it up when ready to serve.

Yield: 6 servings

Summer Sausage

This is good served with polenta and apple sauce or Fried Apple Rings (see page 236).

1   pound unseasoned ground pork
1   bunch mint leaves
1   cup pine nuts
1   green apple
1/4   teaspoon pepper
1   teaspoon salt
zest of 1 lemon

Put the pork in a medium-sized bowl. In a food processor, mince the mint leaves. Add the pine nuts and pulse a few more times. Add this to the pork. Coarsely grate or chop the apple in the food processor. Add the apple, pepper, salt, and lemon zest to the pork and mint mixture. Mix well by hand. Refrigerate for at least 2 hours.

Form into patties and either panfry or brown in a 350° oven on a cookie sheet for 40 minutes. Serve hot.

Yield: 6 servings

Streamliner Buttermilk Waffles

Some mornings at the Streamliner Diner, the craze is waffles. Everyone wants a waffle. Some order waffles two to a stack with fresh sliced strawberries, bananas, or blueberries and whipped cream. We have real maple syrup on hand, too. Some people like their waffles crisp, some like eggs on top, or raisins and nuts mixed into the batter. And there is our dear customer, Cecil, who over the past five years has never ordered anything except a plain golden waffle.

2 *cups unbleached white flour*
2 *teaspoons baking powder*
1 *teaspoon baking soda*
½ *teaspoon salt*
4 *tablespoons butter or margarine*

3 *large eggs*
1½ *cups buttermilk*

Heat up the waffle iron. In a medium-sized bowl, combine the flour, baking powder, baking soda, and salt. Mix thoroughly with a whisk. In a small saucepan, melt the butter or margarine and allow to cool slightly.

Separate the eggs and beat the egg whites until they form stiff peaks. Set aside. In a large bowl, beat the egg yolks with a whisk. Whisk in the buttermilk and the melted butter or margarine. With a large spoon or spatula, stir the dry mix into the wet mix. Avoid overmixing. Fold the egg whites into the batter with a rubber spatula.

Grease the hot waffle iron if necessary. For each waffle, pour onto the waffle iron ¾ cup of the batter and lower the lid. Cook until golden and crisp, approximately 3 minutes. Serve hot with butter and maple syrup or with fruit and whipped cream.

Yield: Four 7-inch waffles

VARIATION

Sprinkle about ¼ cup chopped walnuts, pecans, almonds, or raisins onto the batter just before you lower the waffle iron lid.

Streamliner Granola

Our granola is chock full of almonds and raisins: we serve it with a side of yogurt or milk. Many customers choose to add blueberries or sliced banana as an additional taste treat.

    4 cups rolled oats
    ¾ cup chopped almonds
    ¼ cup water
    ½ cup honey
    2 teaspoons vanilla
    ¾ teaspoon salt
    ½ cup butter or margarine,
        melted
    ¾ cup raisins

Preheat oven to 350°. Mix together the rolled oats and almonds in a large bowl. In a medium-sized bowl, combine the water, honey, vanilla, salt, and melted butter or margarine. Pour this over the oat mixture and stir well. Spread evenly in a 9 × 13-inch baking pan.

Bake at 350° until golden brown, approximately 1 hour. Stir occasionally. Add the raisins after baking. Allow the granola to cool completely, then store it in an airtight container.

Yield: 6 servings

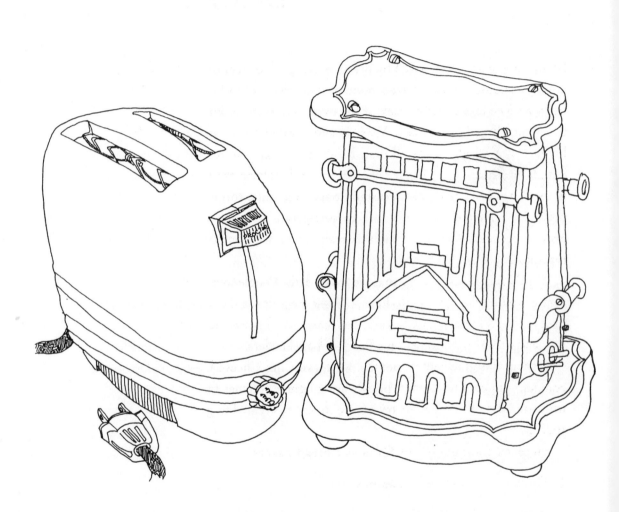

BREADS

Many people are intimidated by bread-making. They feel that yeasted doughs are mysterious, that they have a mind of their own and will stubbornly walk off the job given an untimely crack of the oven or a nasty look from the corner of the room. Breads *are* tricky. Yeast is alive, therefore it can die. But making bread is not as difficult as all that. Most failures are the result of rushing the dough, overheating it to speed the rising, or dissolving the yeast in water that is too hot. Other than that, yeasted doughs are quite forgiving. If timing is a problem, remember that it's safe to refrigerate a dough to slow down the growth process. We have done this many times with our bagel dough at the restaurant.

Bagels are the one bread that we make daily. People love to watch the process of rolling the dough into balls, poking the holes in the middle, and boiling the bagels. When they are baking, the yeasty smell permeates our little restaurant and this usually brings on a flurry of bagel orders.

During the gray winter months, we make Chili Cheese Corn Bread to accompany soups. Our stuffed breads are a lighter summer fare: we serve them with fruit and cheese. Other breads we make are created to go along with daily specials.

Here are some guidelines for novice bread-bakers:

1. Dissolve the yeast in lukewarm water.

2. Add flour a little at a time, usually one cup. This helps prevent toughness.

3. Begin mixing in the flour with a wire whisk or large mixing spoon. Use swift strokes.

4. Once the dough is stiff enough, knead in the rest of the flour, using the palms of your hands, not your fingers. Well-kneaded dough should not be tough or lumpy unless you have added nuts or berries, nor should it be sticky. It should be elastic and as smooth as a baby's bottom. Good dough doesn't resist pressure but gives when poked. It should be "tacky"—it should grab the work surface and let go.

5. Set the dough to rise in a warm, draft-free area. In our restaurant, our bread doughs sometimes rise in 10 to 15 minutes because it is so warm in the kitchen. At home, it will probably take 45 minutes to an hour.

Streamliner Bagels

Our bagels are a great accompaniment to a bowl of soup, a combination ordered every Friday by our carpenter friends, whom we've nicknamed "The Bagel Boys." In the summer, we serve these bagels with smoked salmon, cream cheese, capers, red onions, and tomato slices for a true taste of the Northwest. Just for the record, we know these are not New York bagels.

1 tablespoon active dry yeast

1 cup warm water

½ tablespoon honey or sugar

1 egg

2 tablespoons vegetable oil

1 teaspoon salt

3 to 3½ cups unbleached white flour

1 egg, beaten

Mix the yeast, warm water, and honey or sugar in a large bowl and let stand until it bubbles. Whisk in 1 egg, oil, and salt. Stir in the flour, a little at a time, until the dough is stiff enough to knead. Knead for 8 to 10 minutes, adding flour as needed to keep the dough from sticking. The dough should be smooth and elastic. Put the dough in an oiled bowl. Cover, and set it in a warm, draft-free spot to rise until the dough doubles in size, approximately 30 minutes.

Cut the dough into 6 pieces, and roll each piece into a smooth ball. Using your thumb, poke a hole through the middle of each one. Let sit for 10 minutes. Meanwhile, fill a 4-quart pot half full of water and put it on to boil. Drop the bagels into the water and boil for 1 minute on each side.

Place the bagels on a greased baking sheet and brush them with a beaten egg. Bake in a preheated 400° oven for 20 minutes until tops are golden brown.

Yield: 6 bagels

Molasses Raisin Rolls

When these rolls come out of the oven they smell divine. They are scrumptious eaten hot with a little butter. For an even richer dough, substitute warm milk for the water. We offer these with our Vegetarian Chili (see page 103).

1 tablespoon active dry yeast
1 cup warm water
¼ cup molasses
4 tablespoons butter
2 eggs, beaten
2 teaspoons salt
¾ cup raisins
4 cups unbleached white flour

In a medium-sized bowl, stir together the yeast, water, and molasses. Let stand until it bubbles. Melt and cool the butter. Whisk the butter, eggs, salt, and raisins into the yeast mixture. Stir in flour, a cup at a time, until the dough becomes too stiff to stir with a spoon. Turn the dough out onto your work area, and knead in the rest of the flour until the dough is smooth and elastic. It should grab the work surface, then let go. Clean and oil the mixing bowl. Return the dough to the bowl, cover, and let rise to double in size, approximately 30 minutes.

Grease two 4½ × 8½-inch bread pans. Turn the dough out onto your work area again and cut it into 12 equal-sized pieces. Roll into round balls and set 6 in each greased bread pan. Let rise again for 20 minutes. Bake in a preheated 350° oven for 20 minutes.

Yield: 12 rolls

Great-Grandma's Rye Bread

Judith's Grammy was eating healthily long before it was "in" to do so. She was never one for soft store-bought bread. Here is her recipe for a rye bread that is easy to make and rich and full in flavor.

½ cup butter or margarine
2 yeast cakes or 2 tablespoons
   active dry yeast
¼ cup warm water
approximately 1 cup hot water
1 cup mashed potatoes
½ cup brown sugar

½ cup molasses
4 teaspoons salt
2 tablespoons caraway seeds
2 cups rye flour
3 to 4 cups unbleached white
   flour

Melt the butter or margarine and let it cool. Dissolve the yeast in warm water. Set aside until it bubbles. Add enough hot water to the mashed potatoes to measure 2 cups. In a large bowl, combine yeast and potatoes with butter or margarine, sugar, molasses, salt, and caraway seeds. Start adding flour, 1 cup at a time, until you have a stiff dough. Continue adding smaller amounts until the dough pulls away from the bowl. Knead for 10 minutes. Put the dough in an oiled bowl, cover, and let rise to double its size.

Grease two 4½ × 9-inch bread pans. Form dough into 2 loaves, set in bread pans, and let rise again, about 20 minutes.

Preheat the oven to 425° and bake for 15 minutes. Reduce the temperature to 325° and continue baking for 1 hour. Remove from the oven and butter the tops of the bread.

Yield: 2 loaves

Tomato Herb Braid

Kids love this bread. It smells and tastes like pizza and makes incredibly delicious grilled cheese sandwiches. This dough can also be used for filled breads.

1⅓ cups blended fresh tomatoes

2 tablespoons active dry yeast

1 tablespoon sugar or honey

¾ cup minced onion

3 cloves garlic, minced

4 tablespoons olive oil

¼ cup minced fresh basil

1 teaspoon oregano

1 teaspoon thyme

½ cup grated Parmesan cheese

4 eggs

2½ teaspoons salt

5 to 6 cups unbleached white flour

Heat the blended tomatoes in a small saucepan until lukewarm. Remove from heat and add the yeast and sugar or honey. In a small skillet, sauté the onion and garlic in the olive oil. Let cool. Pour the tomato mixture into a large bowl. Add the onion and garlic. Whisk in the basil, oregano, thyme, Parmesan, 3 of the eggs, and salt. Slowly add the flour while whisking until the dough gets too stiff to whisk. Turn the dough out onto your work area and knead in flour until the dough is smooth and elastic, about 10 minutes. Return the dough to a greased bowl, cover, and let rise to double its size, about 45 minutes.

Grease an 11½ × 17½-inch baking sheet. Braid the dough, set it on the baking sheet, and let rise another 20 to 30 minutes. Beat the remaining egg and brush it on the top of the braid.

Bake in a preheated 350° oven for 30 to 40 minutes, until golden brown on top and a little crispy on the bottom. Let cool thoroughly before serving.

VARIATION

If you want a change of flavor, try 2 teaspoons fennel seed instead of the basil, oregano, and thyme.

Yield: 1 loaf

Kalamata–Feta Cheese–Basil Bread

2 tablespoons active dry yeast

2 tablespoons sugar

2 cups warm water

2 eggs

1 tablespoon salt

¼ cup olive oil

6 cups unbleached white flour

½ cup ricotta cheese

¾ cup crumbled feta cheese

¾ cup chopped and pitted
    Kalamata olives

3 cloves garlic, minced

1 cup chopped fresh basil

½ teaspoon salt

In a medium-sized bowl, combine the yeast, sugar, and warm water. Let stand until it begins to bubble. With a wire whisk, beat in the eggs, salt, and oil. Begin stirring in the flour, a cup at a time, with a large mixing spoon. When the dough gets too stiff to stir, turn it out onto your work area and knead in the rest of the flour, a little at a time. When you have kneaded the rest of the flour in, the dough should be smooth and elastic. Clean and oil the bowl, and return the dough to it. Let the dough rise to double in size, approximately 30 minutes.

Mix the ricotta, feta, olives, garlic, basil, and salt in a small mixing bowl until it is like a paste. Turn the dough out onto your work area. Roll the dough into a ½-inch-thick round with a rolling pin. Spread the cheese and olive paste onto the round. Fold ⅓ of the round back over itself. Take the other edge and fold it overlapping the first edge. Grease an 11½ × 17½-inch baking sheet. Flip the loaf over onto the baking sheet (the edges will be on the bottom). Let rise 15 minutes. Bake for 35 minutes in a preheated 350° oven.

Yield : 1 loaf

VARIATION

To make Blue Cheese–Onion–Thyme Bread, sauté 3 cloves minced garlic, 1½ tablespoons fresh thyme, and 1 diced onion in 1 tablespoon olive oil. When the onion is transparent, remove it from heat and stir in ¾ cup crumbled blue cheese. Use this filling in place of the ricotta-feta-olive combination above.

Walnut–Orange–Anise Bread

½ cup flour
1 tablespoon active dry yeast
½ cup warm water
2 large eggs
3 tablespoons olive oil
⅓ cup honey
1 tablespoon anise or fennel seeds
zest of 1 orange
1½ teaspoons salt
1 cup finely chopped walnuts
2½ cups unbleached white flour

In a small bowl, whisk the flour and yeast together. Add the warm water and whisk again. This is called a sponge. Set the sponge aside and let rise to double its size, approximately 10 minutes. In a medium-sized bowl, whisk the eggs, oil, and honey together in that order. Add the sponge to the eggs and whisk together. In a small skillet set on high heat, toast the anise seeds, stirring constantly until they are light brown. Grind them with a mortar and pestle and add them to the sponge. Add the orange zest, salt, and walnuts, and mix well.

Begin adding flour, a little at a time, with a whisk, until the dough becomes too stiff to stir. Turn it out onto your work area and begin kneading in the rest of the flour until you have incorporated all of it and the dough is smooth and elastic. Clean and oil the bowl. Return the dough to the bowl, cover, and set aside to rise. Let double in size.

Grease a 9×5-inch bread pan. Turn the dough out onto your work area again, and mold it into a loaf. Set it into the bread pan and let rise again until it is ⅓ greater in size. Bake in a preheated 350° oven for 35 to 40 minutes. Let cool thoroughly before cutting.

Yield: 1 loaf

Blackberry Lemon Challah

This is like eating summer itself!

1 cup milk	1½ teaspoons salt
3 tablespoons butter	3 to 3½ cups unbleached white
1 tablespoon active dry yeast	flour
⅓ cup honey	
2 eggs	1 cup blackberries
zest of 1 lemon	1 egg, beaten

Warm the milk in a small saucepan. Add the butter and let it melt. When the butter is melted, pour the milk into a large bowl. Add the yeast and honey and stir to incorporate. Set aside until it bubbles, approximately 10 minutes.

With a wire whisk, beat in 2 eggs, lemon zest, and salt. Begin adding the flour a cup at a time, beating with the whisk until the dough is too stiff to stir. Then turn the dough out onto your work area and knead in the rest of the flour, a little at a time, until all of the flour is incorporated. The dough should be smooth and moist and should grab the work surface, then let go. Clean and grease the mixing bowl. Return the dough to the bowl and cover. Set aside in a warm, draft-free area to rise to double in size. This should take approximately 45 minutes.

Grease an 11 × 17-inch baking sheet. Turn the dough out onto your work area and cut it into 6 equal pieces. Roll each piece into 12- to 15-inch-long ropes. Lay the ropes down vertically next to each other and begin braiding. Lay the braid on the baking sheet. Nestle a blackberry on each apex of the cross sections of the braid. Let rise again for 20 minutes.

Brush the braid with the beaten egg. Bake in a preheated 350° oven for 40 to 50 minutes, until the top is golden brown. Remove and cool.

Yield: 1 loaf

Chili Cheese Corn Bread

Serve this with Vegetarian Chili (see page 103) for a hearty and fulfilling lunch.

1 cup unbleached white flour
1 teaspoon baking soda
2 teaspoons baking powder
3 tablespoons sugar
1 teaspoon salt
²/₃ cup cornmeal
3 eggs, slightly beaten
1 cup buttermilk
3 tablespoons vegetable oil or
   melted butter or margarine

1 cup grated cheddar cheese
½ cup whole kernel corn (frozen
   or canned, well drained)
2 4-ounce cans chopped mild
   green chilies

Preheat oven to 375°. Grease a 9 × 9-inch pan. Mix the flour, baking soda, baking powder, sugar, salt, and cornmeal in a medium-sized bowl. In another medium-sized bowl, combine the eggs, buttermilk, and oil or butter or margarine. Beat with a wire whisk. Make a well in the middle of the dry ingredients. Add the wet ingredients and stir just until the flour is barely moistened. Spread half of the batter in the greased pan. Top with cheese, corn, and green chilies. Pour in the remaining batter.

Bake at 375° for 45 minutes, or until golden brown on top and a toothpick inserted in the middle comes out clean.

Yield: One 9-inch square

SOUPS

We serve soup daily. In the summertime, we make two or three gallons, and in the winter, we make a five-gallon pot. We arrive at the diner early in the morning and assess what we have around to work with. (This is why we half-jokingly say that SOUP stands for Splendid Opportunity to Utilize Potential.) We have already made up our special for the day, so we try to select a soup that will complement it in color, texture, flavor, or ethnic theme. We wouldn't serve a lentil soup with a chili special or a cream soup with a Stroganoff.

The season also influences our planning. Vegetarian Chili rarely shows up in the summer, but is a winter favorite. In the summer, Cold Blueberry Soup and Gazpacho are popular. Each season, we try to take advantage of foods that are available at that time of the year, such as asparagus and nettles in the spring, or wild mushrooms in the autumn.

Sometimes our customers, trusting souls, unknowingly become our co-experimenters as we test out new soups on them. This is how we developed Cold Blueberry Soup and Ribbon-of-the-Sea Soup. We have a regular soup crowd: these folks never bother to inquire—they just order soup for lunch, no matter what it is.

Ribbon-of-the-Sea Soup

Nori is an edible seaweed that comes dried in paper-thin sheets. It can be found in the oriental section of most grocery stores. Nori plays a key role in oriental cuisine. The Japanese eat over 9 billion sheets of this vitamin-rich ocean harvest each year. Its flavor is reminiscent of the salty air and tidal pools along the great Puget Sound.

1 tablespoon butter	4 cups water or vegetable stock
2 tablespoons olive oil	1/4 cup soy sauce
3 cups sliced mushrooms	juice of 1 lemon
1 onion, diced	1/2 teaspoon celery seed
1 stalk celery, diced	1/2 teaspoon salt
2 cloves garlic, minced	1/4 teaspoon black pepper

2 to 3 sheets nori

Heat the butter and oil in a 2-quart saucepan. Sauté the mushrooms until they are limp and start releasing their juices. Add the onion, celery, and garlic and cook over medium heat until the onions are transparent. Add the water or stock, soy sauce, lemon juice, celery seed, salt, and pepper. Cook over medium heat for 30 minutes.

For each serving, tear 1 sheet of nori into strips and pour hot soup over this. Serve at once.

Yield: 2 to 3 servings

VARIATION

Tofu is a lovely addition. To make a hot-and-sour soup, add a few drops each of oriental hot chili oil and sesame oil and 3 tablespoons of lemon juice before serving.

Vegetarian Onion Soup

Like a good cup of coffee, this soup is rich and full-bodied and good to the last drop.

    1½ tablespoons olive oil
    4 cloves garlic, minced
    2 onions, thinly sliced
    1 cup hearty red wine
    1 tablespoon brown sugar or
      molasses
    4 cups water
    2 bay leaves
    2 teaspoons basil
    2 tablespoons soy sauce
    1½ teaspoons salt

Heat the oil in a 3-quart soup pot. Sauté the garlic and onions until the onions become transparent. Continue sautéing on high heat and add the wine and sugar or molasses. When it begins to boil, lower heat and simmer the onions in the wine until they begin breaking down. Add the water, bay leaves, and basil. Return to high heat and bring the soup to a boil. Lower heat, cover, and simmer for 30 minutes. Add the soy sauce and salt. Serve with Herbed Garlic Croutons (see page 133) and Parmesan cheese if desired.

Yield: 3 to 4 servings

Mushroom Barley Soup

2 tablespoons butter

1 tablespoon olive oil

3 cups sliced mushrooms

1 onion, diced

1 stalk celery, diced

1/4 cup dry white wine

2 tablespoons soy sauce

3 1/2 cups water or vegetable stock

1 tablespoon lemon juice

1/2 teaspoon dried dill weed

1/4 cup chopped fresh parsley

1/2 teaspoon celery seed

3/4 teaspoon salt

1/4 teaspoon black pepper

1/4 cup pearl barley

Heat the butter and oil in a 2-quart saucepan. Sauté the mushrooms over high heat until they become limp. Add the onion and celery and cook until the onion becomes transparent. Add the wine and continue cooking over high heat until the wine is reduced to about half. Lower heat to simmer. Add soy sauce and water or stock and simmer for 20 minutes.

Stir in the lemon juice, dill weed, parsley, celery seed, salt, and pepper. Add the barley and simmer for another 40 minutes until the barley is tender.

Yield: 4 to 6 servings

Egg–Onion–Tarragon Soup

1 tablespoon olive oil

2 cloves garlic, minced

1 tablespoon grated fresh ginger

½ onion, diced

1½ cups chopped bok choy

1 cup sliced mushrooms

2½ cups water

1 teaspoon basil

1 teaspoon tarragon

¼ teaspoon black pepper

1 large egg, beaten

½ teaspoon salt

1 tablespoon soy sauce

In a 2-quart saucepan, heat the oil over high heat. Sauté the garlic, ginger, and onion for 2 minutes. Add the bok choy and mushrooms and sauté for 2 more minutes. Add the water, basil, tarragon, and pepper. Cover and bring to a boil. Lower heat and simmer for 15 minutes.

With the soup still simmering, add the egg through a colander or sieve so that the egg cooks in long thin streams on contact with the soup. Add the salt and soy sauce. Let sit a few minutes before serving.

Yield: 2 to 3 servings

Kale–Ham–Bean Soup

Irene discovered this hearty one-dish meal one summer in Provincetown, Massachusetts. Many Portuguese families settled there, at the tip of Cape Cod, for fishing and whaling. This simple country soup of Portuguese origin is delicious and inexpensive to prepare. If kale is unavailable, collard greens may be substituted.

1 cup dry pinto beans	6 cups water
3 cups water	1¼ pounds ham hocks
	1 onion, diced
	2 stalks celery, diced
	1 teaspoon salt
	½ teaspoon black pepper
	1 bunch fresh or frozen kale, chopped

Soak the beans in 3 cups cold water for 4 hours minimum. Drain the soaked beans.

Put the beans, 6 cups water, ham hocks, onion, and celery in a 3-quart pot. Bring to a boil, lower heat, and simmer for 1½ hours until the beans are tender. Remove the meat from the ham hocks and return it to the pot. Add the salt, black pepper, and kale. Cook over medium heat for 25 minutes or until the kale is tender. Serve with Chili Cheese Corn Bread (see page 90) or your favorite crusty bread.

Yield: 4 to 6 servings

Celery and Artichoke Heart Soup

3 8½-ounce cans artichoke
   hearts packed in water
3 tablespoons butter
1 tablespoon olive oil
1 onion, diced
4 stalks celery and tops, diced
2 cloves garlic, minced
¼ cup chopped parsley
4 cups chicken stock
¼ cup lemon juice
1 tablespoon dried dill weed
½ teaspoon celery seed
1 teaspoon salt
½ teaspoon black pepper

2 tablespoons cornstarch
¼ cup cold water

Drain and finely chop the artichoke hearts. Heat the butter and oil in a 3-quart soup pot. Sauté the onion and celery until the onion is transparent. Add the garlic, parsley and artichoke hearts. Sauté another 3 minutes. Add the chicken stock, lemon juice, dill weed, celery seed, salt, and pepper. Cover and bring to a boil. Lower heat and simmer for 30 minutes.

Mix the cornstarch and water. Add it to the soup, stirring constantly until the cornstarch clears and the soup thickens.

Yield: 4 servings

Tomato Bacon Soup

This simple combination of tomatoes, bacon, and onions creates a mouth-watering comfort soup.

6 slices bacon, diced
1 onion, diced
1 46-ounce can tomato juice
¼ cup polenta or cornmeal
juice of 1 lemon
1 teaspoon salt
½ teaspoon black pepper

In a 2-quart pot, fry the bacon until lightly browned. Drain off most of the fat. Add the onion and sauté over medium heat until the onion is transparent. Add the tomato juice. Heat to a simmer. Add the polenta or cornmeal, stirring to avoid lumps. Cook until the cereal is done, approximately 25 minutes, stirring occasionally. Add the lemon juice, salt, and black pepper and serve.

Yield: 4 servings

Spicy Tomato–Nut–Rice Stew

This is a favorite among our customers, especially for the lovers of spicy hot foods.

¼ cup butter

2 tablespoons olive oil

3 cloves garlic, minced

1 onion, diced

1 potato, diced

1 green pepper, diced

1 large tomato, diced

4 cups chicken stock

½ teaspoon finely chopped
jalapeño (optional)

¼ teaspoon cayenne pepper

¼ teaspoon black pepper

1 bay leaf

¼ cup uncooked white rice

¼ cup crunchy peanut butter

1 teaspoon salt

1½ tablespoons honey

¼ cup roasted peanuts

¼ cup fresh cilantro leaves

Heat the butter and oil in a 3-quart soup pot and sauté the garlic and onion on high heat until the onion becomes transparent. Add the potato, green pepper, and tomato and sauté 5 more minutes. Add the chicken stock. Cover and bring soup to a boil. Lower heat, add the optional jalapeño, cayenne, black pepper, and bay leaf and simmer for 15 minutes. Wash the rice under cold water, then add it to the soup pot and simmer another 15 to 20 minutes, stirring occasionally to prevent the rice from sticking.

Ladle 1 cup of the soup stock into medium-sized bowl. Add the peanut butter and stir until it is dissolved. Return to the pot. Stir in the salt and honey. Cook on low heat another 10 minutes.

Mince the peanuts and cilantro to use as garnish on the soup. Serve hot.

Yield: 4 to 6 servings

Tortilla Soup

Have you ever wondered what to do with those old stale tortilla chips that you just hate to dump out? Well here's how to revive them in a most delicious way.

1 tablespoon butter or margarine

2 tablespoons olive oil

1 onion, diced

3 cloves garlic, minced

1 carrot, diced

1 green pepper, diced

2 stalks celery, diced

4 cups tomato juice

1½ cups water

1 4-ounce can chopped green chilies

3 tablespoons lemon juice

3 tablespoons salsa, or 1 tablespoon minced jalapeños, 2 teaspoons oregano, and 2 teaspoons cumin

2 cups tortilla chips

2 tablespoons chopped fresh cilantro

Heat the butter or margarine and olive oil in a 3-quart pot and sauté the onion and garlic until transparent. Add the carrot, green pepper, and celery. Sauté for 1 minute. Add the tomato juice, water, and green chilies. Cover and cook over medium heat for 25 minutes until vegetables are tender.

Lower heat. Stir in the lemon juice and salsa or jalapeños, oregano, and cumin. Crush the tortilla chips. Add 1 cup of the tortilla chips to the soup and let sit 10 minutes. Just before serving, garnish each bowl with several crushed tortilla chips and a sprinkle of cilantro.

Yield: 4 to 6 servings

Vegetarian Chili

1 cup dry pinto beans

4 cups water

4 tablespoons olive oil

1 onion, diced

4 cloves garlic, minced

1 green pepper, diced

1 cup sliced black olives

4 Roma tomatoes, chopped

½ cup hearty red wine

1½ teaspoons cumin

2 bay leaves

2 dashes Tabasco sauce

½ teaspoon red chili pepper
flakes (optional)

2 tablespoons molasses

1½ teaspoons salt

Put the beans in a 2-quart soup pot with 4 cups of water. Cover and bring to a boil. Lower heat and simmer for 45 minutes.

In a large skillet, heat the oil and sauté the onion, garlic, green pepper, olives, and tomatoes until the onion is transparent. Add this to the cooked beans along with the wine, cumin, bay leaves, Tabasco, optional chili flakes, molasses, and salt. Cook another 30 minutes.

Note: We serve this with Molasses Raisin Rolls (see page 84). The combination makes a fine autumn mid-afternoon meal. It's also good with Chili Cheese Corn Bread (see page 90).

Yield: 3 to 4 servings

Spicy Bouillabaisse

This is our exciting rendition of bouillabaisse. It receives high praise at the Streamliner every time we serve it. The addition of orange zest and fennel sets it apart from the typical version of this seafood stew.

4 tablespoons olive oil

4 cloves garlic, minced

1 onion, diced

1 potato, diced

1 green pepper, diced

4 Roma tomatoes, diced

1½ teaspoons fennel seeds

2 teaspoons orange zest

2 bay leaves

¼ teaspoon black pepper

⅛ teaspoon cayenne pepper (optional)

½ cup red wine

4 cups clam nectar

1½ teaspoons salt

1 tablespoon honey

¾ pound shucked steamer clams

1 pound Alaskan cod, in chunks

½ pound prawns, shelled and deveined

1½ teaspoons fresh fennel, minced

Heat the oil in a 3-quart soup pot on high heat. Sauté the garlic, onion, potato, green pepper, and tomatoes in that order, approximately 2 minutes each, or until the onion and potato are transparent. Add the fennel seeds, orange zest, bay leaves, black and cayenne peppers, and red wine. Continue on high heat and let the wine cook off almost completely. Add the clam nectar. Bring to a boil. Lower heat and let simmer for 15 minutes. Add the salt and honey.

Five minutes before serving, add the clams, cod, and prawns. Cover and turn the heat off. Let the seafood cook in the hot broth for 5 to 10 minutes. Serve immediately, garnished with fennel.

Yield: 4 to 6 servings

Doukhobor Borscht

The Doukhobors are a Christian group that originated in Russia in the mid-1700s. In the late 1800s the Doukhobors adopted many ideas of Leo Tolstoy. It was with the help of Tolstoy and English and American Quakers that 7,000 Doukhobors immigrated to western Canada, where they established communal farms. This recipe was gleaned from a friend in Vancouver whose grandmother is a Doukhobor. The soup is rich and hearty and can easily constitute a complete meal when served with bread.

2 beets	1 cup half-and-half
1 potato, diced	2 teaspoons dried dill weed
3 cups water	2 tablespoons butter
	1 teaspoon salt
2 tablespoons butter	1 tomato, diced
1/4 cup diced carrot	
1/2 cup shredded cabbage	1/2 cup sour cream
1/4 cup diced green pepper	

In a 2-quart pot, boil the whole beets in water to cover for 25 minutes. Trim off the tops and bottoms, slip off the skins, and dice the beets. In a small pot, boil the diced potato in 3 cups of water for 10 minutes and set aside.

Melt 2 tablespoons butter in a 2-quart pot. Sauté the carrot, cabbage, and green pepper in the butter for 5 minutes. Add half of the cooked potato and all of the liquid that the potato was cooked in to the pot of sautéed vegetables.

Mash the other half of the potato with the half-and-half, dill, 2 tablespoons butter, and salt. Add the mashed potato, beets, and tomato to the soup and cook over low heat for 30 minutes, taking care not to boil.

To serve, garnish each bowl of soup with a large dollop of sour cream.

Yield: 4 to 6 servings

Carrot Fennel Soup

This soup is very light and flavorful—great served with rye bread and a hearty salad.

1 large potato, diced
2 carrots, diced
1 onion, diced
½ large fresh fennel bulb and
   stalk, minced
1 clove garlic, minced
1 bay leaf
4 cups water

juice and zest of 1 orange
3 tablespoons honey
½ teaspoon turmeric
⅛ teaspoon nutmeg
½ teaspoon cinnamon
½ teaspoon curry powder
½ teaspoon celery seed
1 tablespoon salt
½ teaspoon black pepper
½ teaspoon thyme
pinch of cayenne pepper

1 cup half-and-half

In a 3-quart pot, bring to a boil the potato, carrots, onion, fennel (save some tops for garnish), garlic, and bay leaf in 4 cups of water. Cover, lower heat, and simmer until the vegetables are tender. Blend these ingredients in a food processor or blender until smooth.

Return the blended ingredients to the pot and stir in the orange juice and zest, honey, and all the seasonings. Stir in the half-and-half. Make sure not to boil the soup at this point. Keep the heat low until ready to serve. Garnish with reserved minced fennel tops.

Yield: 4 to 6 servings

Cream of Wild Mushroom Soup

Hunting for wild mushrooms is a favorite fall pastime in the Northwest. When the rains begin, they soak the ground and bring forth such wonderful edible fungi as chanterelles, meadow mushrooms, and shaggy manes. If wild mushrooms are not available, you can make this soup with domestic mushrooms. It will be very good, but somewhat milder in flavor.

1/4 cup butter

2 tablespoons olive oil

1 pound wild or domestic mushrooms, sliced (6 cups)

1 cup chicken stock

4 cups milk

4 tablespoons butter, room temperature

4 tablespoons flour

1 teaspoon dried dill weed

2 teaspoons salt

1/2 teaspoon pepper

Heat the butter and oil in a large, heavy frying pan. Add the mushrooms and sauté until the mushrooms release their juices. Add the chicken stock. When the stock begins bubbling, lower the heat, cover, and simmer for 30 minutes.

Meanwhile, in a 3-quart pot, heat the milk but keep it below the boiling point. In a small bowl, knead together the butter and flour with your fingers until a smooth paste is formed. Stir some hot milk into the flour-butter mixture and stir until smooth. Add this paste back to the hot milk, stirring to incorporate the flour and butter. Continue cooking until it begins to thicken. Add the mushrooms, dill weed, salt, and pepper and cook on low heat for a few minutes. Do not let the soup boil, as it could curdle. Correct the seasonings to taste. Serve hot with a fresh, crusty bread.

Yield: 4 to 6 servings

Winslow Clam Chowder

Every cookbook from the Pacific Northwest must have a recipe for clam chowder. Here's our contribution from deep in the heart of Winslow, the only town on Bainbridge Island.

3 tablespoons butter, or 2 slices bacon

1 onion, diced

2 stalks celery, diced

2 potatoes, diced

¼ cup flour

3 cups water or chicken stock

¼ cup minced parsley

1 teaspoon salt

1 teaspoon black pepper

1 cup fresh or canned chopped clams

1½ cups half-and-half or milk

1 dab butter per serving

¼ cup minced parsley, or ½ cup Herbed Garlic Croutons (see page 133)

Dice bacon if you are using bacon. In a 2-quart pot, cook the bacon until it begins releasing juices or melt 3 tablespoons of butter. Sauté the onion and celery until the onion is transparent. Add the diced potatoes and heat through. Add the flour and stir. The flour will get a little sticky on the bottom of the pot, so keep stirring for a minute. Add water or chicken stock and parsley and stir until smooth. Cook until the potatoes are tender, about 20 minutes, stirring occasionally to prevent sticking.

Add salt, black pepper, clams, and half-and-half or milk. Cook over low heat, taking care not to boil, until the soup is heated through.

To serve, put a pat of butter in each bowl, ladle in the hot soup, and garnish with parsley or Herbed Garlic Croutons.

Yield: 4 to 6 servings

Curried Parsley and Potato Soup

This is one of our tastiest vegetarian soups. You can use milk instead of cream, or, if you are really watching your cholesterol intake, just use potatoes as a thickener. This soup is also excellent made with chicken stock.

2 tablespoons olive oil or butter	2 bunches parsley, sprigs only
3 cloves garlic, minced	⅔ cup water
½ onion, diced	
3 potatoes, diced	1⅓ cups cream or milk
2 teaspoons curry powder	1 teaspoon salt
¼ cup Worcestershire sauce	pinch of pepper
4 cups water	

Heat the oil or butter over high heat in a 3-quart soup pot. Sauté the garlic, onion, and potatoes until the onion and potatoes become transparent. Add the curry powder, Worcestershire sauce, and water. Cover and bring to a boil. Lower heat and simmer for 30 minutes.

Meanwhile, purée the parsley sprigs and water in a blender. The purée will be like a thin pesto. Set aside.

Remove soup from heat. Blend it in a blender or food processor until creamy and return it to the pot. Add the parsley mixture, stir, and return soup to the stove on low heat. Add the cream or milk, salt, and pepper to taste. Heat the soup through, but do not bring it to a boil.

Yield: 4 to 6 servings

Gazpacho

1 onion

2 cloves garlic

1 green pepper

1 cucumber, peeled

3 tomatoes

2 stalks celery

3 green onions

1 46-ounce can tomato juice

¼ cup olive oil

½ cup seasoned bread crumbs

4 tablespoons lime juice

2 teaspoons salt

½ teaspoon Tabasco sauce

pepper to taste

In a food processor, finely chop the onion, garlic, green pepper, cucumber, and tomatoes. Pour this mixture into a 4-quart container. Finely dice the celery and green onions and add to the other vegetables. Stir in the tomato juice, olive oil, bread crumbs, lime juice, salt, Tabasco sauce, and pepper to taste. Cover and chill thoroughly before serving.

Yield: 6 servings

Chilled Blueberry Soup

This unusual soup titillates the taste buds and cools the body on a hot summer's day.

4 cups blueberries, fresh or frozen	1 cup uncooked egg noodles
3 cups water	¼ cup sour cream
juice and zest of 1 lemon	
½ cup sugar	
⅛ teaspoon cinnamon	
⅛ teaspoon salt	
2 tablespoons cornstarch	
¼ cup water	

In a 2-quart saucepan, bring the blueberries, water, lemon juice and zest, sugar, cinnamon, and salt to a boil over high heat. Lower heat and simmer for 3 minutes. Dissolve cornstarch in ¼ cup cold water. Add to the soup and cook another 5 minutes, until the cornstarch clears.

In a small saucepan, cook the noodles in boiling salted water for 6 to 8 minutes. Drain. Rinse. Add the noodles to the soup and chill for 3 to 4 hours. Garnish each serving with 1 tablespoon of sour cream.

Yield: 3 to 4 servings

SALADS

Each morning in the restaurant we plan a salad to accompany our daily special. This requires flexibility and creativity: we want the salad to complement the foods we are serving, but at the same time we are limited by what is in season at any given time, and by what is on hand.

We frequently purchase our produce at the supermarket next door—it has an impressive variety of fresh vegetables and herbs, many of them organic. The market buys as much as it can from local farmers, so we are often able to use produce grown right here on Bainbridge Island.

We think of salads as the chameleon of foods. They adapt to any need the cook may have. They can be an addition to a meal or a meal in themselves. And they can be made with just about any ingredients whatsoever. The magic of a good salad is in the dressing. Whether it is simple and subtle or loud and demanding, a good dressing should both complement and enhance the salad.

Wilted Spinach Salad

2 bunches spinach, washed
2 tablespoons sesame seeds

2 tablespoons rice vinegar
1 tablespoon sugar
1 tablespoon soy sauce
1 tablespoon dark sesame oil
½ teaspoon salt

Bring 2 quarts water to a boil. Add the spinach to the boiling water to wilt it and drain it immediately. Chill under cold running water or in an ice water bath and squeeze dry gently. Put it in a medium-sized bowl and set aside.

In a small, heavy skillet, brown the sesame seeds on medium-high heat until they begin popping. Remove and set aside.

To make the dressing, mix together the rice vinegar, sugar, soy sauce, sesame oil, and salt in a small bowl. Toss the spinach with the dressing. Refrigerate until well chilled. Serve topped with the sesame seeds.

Yield: 2 to 3 servings

Kindling Carrots

1 bunch spinach or watercress   toasted almonds
4 large carrots

3 cloves garlic, minced
¼ cup diced green pepper
¼ cup olive oil
¼ teaspoon hot chili oil
¼ cup cider or wine vinegar
1 tablespoon honey
1 teaspoon orange zest
1 teaspoon salt

Wash the spinach leaves or watercress and pat dry.

Peel the carrots and julienne them.

Steam the carrots for 4 to 5 minutes in a steamer, or cook them in a small saucepan with ½ inch of water and a pinch of salt. They should be bright orange and a little bit crunchy when they are done. Chill in the refrigerator for 30 minutes.

To make the dressing, put the garlic, green pepper, two oils, vinegar, honey, orange zest, and salt in a blender or food processor. Blend until smooth and creamy.

Toss the dressing with the carrots. Serve on a bed of spinach or watercress. Garnish with toasted almonds.

Yield: 4 servings

Sumi Salad

6 ounces wide egg noodles

1 or 2 teaspoons vegetable oil

1 head Napa cabbage (Chinese cabbage)

1 8-ounce can sliced water chestnuts

4 green onions, sliced diagonally

½ cup toasted chopped almonds

⅓ cup vegetable oil

½ cup rice vinegar

3 cloves garlic, minced

3 tablespoons honey

1½ teaspoons salt

½ teaspoon pepper

2 teaspoons dark sesame oil

In a large pot, bring 2 to 3 quarts of lightly salted water to a rolling boil. Add the noodles and cook until al dente, about 10 to 12 minutes. Drain the noodles, rinse them in cold water, and drain again. Put the noodles in a medium-sized bowl, oil lightly, and chill.

Fill a 4-quart saucepan half full of lightly salted water and put it on to boil. Shred the Napa cabbage and drop it into the boiling water for 2 minutes. Transfer to a colander and drain.

In a small bowl, whisk together ⅓ cup vegetable oil, vinegar, garlic, honey, salt, pepper, and sesame oil.

Add the water chestnuts, green onions, and Napa cabbage to the noodles and mix. Toss the salad with the dressing and chill for at least 1 hour. Toss with the toasted almonds just before serving.

Yield: 4 servings

Spanish Flag Salad

This red, white, and green salad is served warm or at room temperature. It is a great accompaniment to grilled meat or fish, or serve it as a vegetarian main dish along with a hefty bread or a grain dish.

¼ cup olive oil

1 onion, sliced ¼ inch thick

1 eggplant, julienned

1 sweet red pepper, sliced ¼ inch thick

2 green peppers, sliced ¼ inch thick

2 cloves garlic

3 tablespoons lemon juice

2 tablespoons capers

2 tablespoons olive oil

salt and black pepper to taste

½ cup Kalamata olives, pitted

Grease a 9½ × 13-inch baking pan with a little olive oil. In a large bowl toss the onion and eggplant with 2 tablespoons of the olive oil. Spread the onion and eggplant on the pan, cover, and bake at 350° for 45 minutes.

Spread 2 tablespoons of olive oil in another baking pan and add the peppers and whole garlic cloves. Cover and bake for 30 minutes. Remove the garlic and reserve.

Mix all the vegetables together and bake uncovered until the eggplant starts to brown, approximately 25 minutes.

To prepare the dressing, mash the reserved garlic cloves and combine them with the lemon juice, capers, 2 tablespoons olive oil, and salt and black pepper. Toss the vegetables with the dressing. Add the olives. Serve either warm or at room temperature.

Note: With feta cheese, this dish can also be used as a calzone filling (see page 152).

Yield: 4 to 6 servings

Russian Vegetable Salad

This salad is one element of the traditional spreads that Irene remembers from her childhood family gatherings on Long Island. The European fare also included roast beef, Danish herring salad, and Grandma's Potato Salad (see page 119).

2 medium beets

2 medium new potatoes

2 carrots, diced

1 cup fresh or frozen petite peas

$\frac{1}{2}$ cup mayonnaise

3 tablespoons lemon juice

1 teaspoon dried dill weed

$\frac{1}{2}$ teaspoon salt

$\frac{1}{4}$ teaspoon pepper

$\frac{3}{4}$ cup diced sweet pickles

$1\frac{1}{2}$ tablespoons capers (optional)

Cook the whole beets in water to cover until barely tender, about 30 minutes. Run the beets under cold water, slip off the skins, and cut the beets into $\frac{1}{2}$-inch dice.

In a medium-sized pot, cover the new potatoes with water and boil until just tender, about 30 minutes. After the potatoes have cooked for 25 minutes, add the diced carrots to the pot. When the potatoes are done, remove them from the pot. Add the peas to the pot and simmer with the carrots for 3 minutes. Drain the carrots and peas. When the potatoes are cool, dice them.

To make the dressing, whisk together the mayonnaise, lemon juice, dill weed, salt, and pepper in a small bowl.

In a medium-sized serving bowl, combine the beets, potatoes, carrots, and peas with the sweet pickles and the optional capers. Toss with the dressing. Chill for a few hours before serving.

Yield: 4 to 6 servings

Grandma's Potato Salad

People always wonder what is different about this potato salad. Apples, we tell them. This salad has tang and crunch, and is a favorite among our customers. It improves over time, too, so if there is some left over, don't fret. In fact, we often purposely make more than we need. This is another recipe we inherited from Irene's grandma.

5 medium new potatoes
2 stalks celery, diced
1 onion, diced
2 tablespoons chopped parsley

¼ cup olive oil
¼ cup wine or cider vinegar
½ teaspoon dried dill weed
1 teaspoon salt
½ teaspoon pepper
¼ teaspoon celery seed

½ cup mayonnaise
½ cup yogurt
½ cup chopped dill pickle
1 green apple, diced
1 tablespoon prepared mustard
1 tablespoon sugar (optional)
salt, pepper, and vinegar to taste

Steam the potatoes for approximately 30 minutes. Cool, peel, and thinly slice them. In a large bowl, combine the potatoes with the celery, onion, and parsley.

In a small bowl, whisk together the olive oil, vinegar, dill weed, salt, pepper, and celery seed. Toss with the potatoes and refrigerate for a few hours or overnight.

To prepare the dressing, combine the mayonnaise, yogurt, pickle, apple, mustard, and optional sugar in a small bowl. Before serving, combine the marinated vegetables with the dressing. Correct the seasonings to taste.

Yield: 4 to 6 servings

Jicama Salad
(Rooster's Beak)

Gerardo, a special Streamliner Diner friend, introduced us to this salad, a cool favorite among his friends in Mexico. This dish is served along with other finger foods and drinks at weekend get-togethers. It is very crunchy and refreshing.

1 pound jicama, peeled and
   julienned
1 sweet red pepper, cut in strips
½ bunch cilantro, leaves only

zest and juice of 1 lime
⅛ teaspoon salt
1 tablespoon sugar

Mix the jicama and sweet red pepper with the cilantro leaves. Combine the lime zest and juice with the salt and sugar. Toss all the ingredients together and chill until ready to serve.

Note: You can adjust the flavors by adding more lime juice or sugar to taste.

Yield: 3 to 4 servings

Streamliner Gazpacho Salad

Liz first tasted gazpacho salad at a friend's wedding. This is her variation on a refreshing theme of crunchy vegetables and herbs. It's topped with Herbed Garlic Croutons.

1 small red pepper, julienned
1 small green pepper, julienned
3 tomatoes, cut into wedges
1 large cucumber, peeled and diced
½ red onion, thinly sliced
2 green onions, finely chopped

¼ cup olive oil
3 tablespoons red wine vinegar
juice and zest of ½ lemon
2 cloves garlic, minced
¼ teaspoon cumin
½ teaspoon tarragon
½ teaspoon basil
½ teaspoon honey
1 dash Tabasco sauce
¼ cup minced parsley

1 cup Herbed Garlic Croutons
(see page 133)

In a large bowl, toss together the peppers, tomatoes, cucumber, and red and green onions.

Mix the oil, vinegar, lemon juice and zest, garlic, cumin, tarragon, basil, honey, Tabasco sauce, and parsley in a small bowl with a wire whisk. Pour the dressing over the salad and toss. Chill for at least 2 hours. Just before serving, top with Herbed Garlic Croutons.

Yield: 4 to 6 servings

Lentil–Feta Cheese–Caper Salad

2 cups dry lentils (5½ cups cooked)

1 carrot
1 bunch green onions, chopped
1 bunch parsley, chopped
1½ cups crumbled feta cheese
4 tablespoons capers

2 eggs
3 cloves garlic, minced
½ cup lemon juice
½ cup olive oil
1 teaspoon salt
½ teaspoon pepper
1 teaspoon anchovy paste

Put dry lentils in a 2-quart saucepan or soup pot and add water to 1½ inches above the lentils. Cover and bring to a boil on high heat. Lower heat and simmer for 30 minutes. Remove from heat. Drain and chill for 1 hour.

Peel and julienne the carrot. Cook in a steamer for 4 to 5 minutes. It should be bright orange and still a little crunchy. Rinse under cold water to cool. Put the carrots in a medium-sized salad bowl with the lentils, green onions, parsley, feta cheese, and capers. Toss.

To make the dressing, beat the eggs with a wire whisk in a small mixing bowl. Add the garlic, lemon juice, oil, salt, pepper, and anchovy paste. Beat with the wire whisk until well blended. Toss the dressing with the lentils and vegetables.

Yield: 4 to 6 servings

Mushroom–Bacon–Blue Cheese Salad

The combination of flavors in this salad, once tasted, produces the Pavlovian response whenever the name is mentioned. The crisp romaine lettuce, bacon, blue cheese, and ambrosial marinated mushrooms, all tossed with a Dijon vinaigrette, make for an elegant salad.

1 cup mushrooms
1 tablespoon butter
1 tablespoon soy sauce
1 tablespoon dry cooking sherry
3 slices bacon

1 head romaine lettuce, torn
½ cup crumbled blue cheese
1 cup walnut halves, toasted
¾ cup Herbed Garlic Croutons
   (see page 133)

¼ cup lemon juice
1 tablespoon Dijon mustard
2 cloves garlic, minced
½ teaspoon Worcestershire sauce
½ teaspoon salt
¼ teaspoon pepper
½ cup olive oil

Clean the mushrooms with a brush. Heat the butter, soy sauce, and sherry in a 2-quart saucepan. Add the mushrooms, cover, and bring to a boil. Drain the mushrooms, reserving the juices to use in soups or sauces. Let the mushrooms cool.

Cube the bacon. Brown it in a frying pan and drain.

To make the dressing in a blender or food processor, combine the lemon juice, mustard, garlic, Worcestershire sauce, salt, and pepper. Slowly drizzle in the olive oil with the blender or processor running. If using a whisk, just whisk together the ingredients in the same order.

To arrange the salad, start with a bed of romaine, then add the mushrooms, blue cheese, bacon, walnuts, and croutons, in that order. Top with the dressing and serve.

Yield: 4 servings

Blue Cheese–Pear–Walnut Salad

The tangy sweetness of the dressing, mixed with the salty flavor of blue cheese and the nuts, entices you to eat more.

1 Bartlett pear, cored and sliced
   lengthwise in thin strips
¾ cup crumbled blue cheese
¾ cup walnut halves, toasted
8 large romaine leaves, torn

¼ cup olive oil
¼ cup cider vinegar
3 cloves garlic, minced
5 large basil leaves, minced
1 teaspoon salt
1 tablespoon honey

Mix the pear, cheese, walnuts, and romaine in a medium-sized salad bowl.

To make the dressing, stir the oil, vinegar, garlic, basil, salt, and honey in a small bowl with a wire whisk. Toss the dressing with the salad just before serving.

Yield: 4 servings

Curried Chicken Salad

This favorite summer salad is crunchy and tangy, a refreshing combination of flavors. You can also serve it as a sandwich in pocket bread, omitting the romaine lettuce.

½ pound or 1 cup chicken, cooked and diced

½ head romaine lettuce, torn

½ tart green apple, diced

2 stalks celery, diced

⅓ cup raisins

⅓ cup sliced dried apricots (optional)

⅓ cup toasted chopped almonds

½ cup mayonnaise

½ cup yogurt

2 teaspoons curry powder

juice of ½ lemon

2 tablespoons honey

almond slivers

In a large bowl, mix the chicken, romaine, apple, celery, raisins, optional apricots, and chopped almonds.

To prepare the dressing, mix the mayonnaise, yogurt, curry, lemon, and honey in a separate bowl with a wire whisk. Toss the salad with the dressing. Top with a few almond slivers.

Yield: 4 to 6 servings

Wild Greens Bouquet

In May, the garden is a feast of scents, tastes, and visual delights. Sally forth into your garden with a basket under your arm. Pick fresh tarragon, the leaves of baby spinach and Swiss chard, and feathery sprigs of florence or bronze fennel. Gathering the greens and the bouquet of edible flowers is as pleasurable as assembling these ingredients into a wildly colorful salad. The Orange Tarragon Vinaigrette, drizzled on top, binds together the flavors, making this spring garden salad a feast for the mouth as well as for the eyes.

24 asparagus spears	6 calendula flowers (orange)
	6 chervil blossoms (white)
½ pound spinach leaves	6 mustard flowers (yellow)
6 Swiss chard leaves	12 onion blossoms (pink)
3 ounces watercres	24 borage blossoms (purple)
½ ounce fresh fennel	12 sprigs fresh tarragon
	6 Swiss chard leaves
	Orange Tarragon Vinaigrette
	(recipe follows)

Steam the asparagus spears in a vegetable steamer until just tender, approximately 5 minutes. Set aside to cool.

Wash and dry the spinach, Swiss chard, and watercress. Tear the spinach and 6 Swiss chard leaves into bite-sized pieces. Pinch the fennel into individual filaments, and toss it together with the spinach, Swiss chard, and watercress in a large salad bowl.

Separate the calendula petals and the chervil and mustard florettes. Arrange them on top of the greens to create a bouquet of color. Strategically place the onion and borage blossoms, the steamed asparagus spears, and the tarragon sprigs on top of the greens. Place 6 Swiss chard leaves around the rim of the salad bowl. Drizzle Orange Tarragon Vinaigrette over the salad before serving.

Yield: 6 servings

Orange Tarragon Vinaigrette

Orange Tarragon Vinaigrette can be served with a variety of green salads. Originally, Liz and Judith created this recipe for the Wild Greens Bouquet (see preceding recipe).

1 cup olive oil	zest of 1 orange, minced
½ cup red wine vinegar	½ teaspoon salt
1 ounce fresh tarragon leaves	⅛ teaspoon pepper
2 tablespoons orange juice concentrate	1 tablespoon honey

Combine all the ingredients in a blender and blend until smooth. Refrigerate.

Yield: 1¾ cups

Creamy Basil Garlic Dressing

This dressing is the house dressing we serve most frequently on our green salads. The other house dressings that we serve often are: Lemon Tahini, Blue Cheese, and Tangy Beer.

1 cup buttermilk	2 cloves garlic, minced
¼ cup sour cream	2 teaspoons basil
½ cup mayonnaise	pinch of salt

With a wire whisk, mix together buttermilk, sour cream, mayonnaise, garlic, basil, and salt in a small bowl. Refrigerate.

Yield: 1¾ cups

Blue Cheese Dressing

1 clove garlic	¼ teaspoon pepper
¼ cup red wine vinegar	½ cup sour cream
1 tablespoon honey	1 cup crumbled blue cheese

Mince the garlic in a blender or food processor. Add the vinegar, honey, pepper, and sour cream. Blend until smooth. Stir in the blue cheese with a mixing spoon, allowing some of the cheese to stay in small pieces. Refrigerate.

Yield: 1½ cups

Tangy Beer Dressing

Our Tangy Beer Dressing has an unusual combination of flavors. This dressing is delicious on a spinach salad.

¾ cup mayonnaise	2 teaspoons horseradish
¼ cup Dijon mustard	pinch of salt
3 ounces light beer (⅜ cup)	

With a wire whisk, mix together the mayonnaise, Dijon mustard, beer, horseradish, and salt in a small bowl. Refrigerate.

Yield: 1⅓ cups

Caesar Salad Dressing
(Caesar Salad)

For a classic Caesar salad, toss this versatile dressing with torn romaine leaves, grated Parmesan cheese, an egg yolk, and Herbed Garlic Croutons (see page 133).

¾ cup olive oil	1 teaspoon salt
½ cup lemon juice	½ teaspoon pepper
3 cloves garlic	10 anchovy fillets

Blend the olive oil, lemon juice, garlic, salt, pepper, and anchovy fillets in a food processor or blender until smooth. Refrigerate.

Yield: 1¾ cups

Lemon Tahini Dressing

Tahini is a paste made of ground sesame seeds. It is used in many Middle Eastern dishes such as hummus or baba ghanouj. This dressing can also be used as a sauce for grains or a dip for vegetables. It will keep refrigerated for up to two weeks.

3 cloves garlic	1 cup tahini
⅔ cup lemon juice, preferably fresh	zest of 1 lemon, minced
¼ cup vinegar	1 tablespoon dried dill weed
¼ cup water	1 teaspoon salt

Mince the garlic in a blender or food processor. Add the lemon juice, vinegar, water, and tahini. Blend until smooth. Add the lemon zest, dill weed, and salt. Blend for 1 more minute. Refrigerate.

Yield: 2 cups

Basil–Lime–Avocado Dressing

1 avocado
1 cup chopped fresh basil
zest and juice of 2 limes
¼ cup rice vinegar

½ cup water
1½ teaspoons salt
1 tablespoon honey

Combine the avocado and basil in a blender or food processor and blend until creamy. Mince the zest and add it and the remaining ingredients to the avocado. Blend again until creamy. Refrigerate.

Yield: 2 cups

Herbed Garlic Croutons

These croutons make good use of bread ends and other odd pieces of stale bread. They are delicious in soups and salads.

½ cup butter or margarine	1 teaspoon thyme
3 cloves garlic, minced	10 pieces of bread or bread ends,
1 teaspoon oregano	cubed
1 teaspoon basil	

Preheat oven to 350°. In a small saucepan, melt the butter or margarine. Stir the garlic, oregano, basil, and thyme into the melted butter or margarine. Place the cubed bread in a 9 × 11-inch pan. Pour the butter or margarine mixture over the bread, and toss to coat.

Bake at 350° for 45 minutes, or until the croutons are crisp, stirring occasionally. Cool and store in an airtight container until ready for use.

Yield: 5 cups

SPECIALS

Every day we offer one special dish that is not on the regular menu. These "specials" fulfill several needs. They allow us a creative avenue outside the limitations of a fixed menu and they provide our regular customers with a change of scenery, so to speak. They also allow us to take advantage of the seasonal availability of ingredients.

In the preparation of our daily specials, we have the opportunity to play. We travel around the world through our foods, experimenting with spices and foods of other lands. We also enjoy standard American fare from all over the country.

We plan our menu a week ahead of time at the weekly business meeting of the four partners. Since one of us is in the diner cooking almost every day we decide what we feel like cooking on our days. We consider food on hand that must be used. We maintain a balance of vegetarian and meat dishes throughout the week. We also think about the ethnicity of our dishes and avoid planning Mexican dishes eight days a week. Our planning has no pattern and the goal is to repeat specials infrequently. When we get bored with our repertoire, we just make up new recipes. We have to give credit to some of our customers who are courageous pioneers, trying anything we make, even if it sounds strange, like the Artichoke Heart–Brie Turnovers or Chicken Liver Spiedini!

We do use cookbooks to get ideas, but rarely are recipes adhered to. If used at all, they function merely as a guideline or as a foundation upon which to elaborate. We tend to find most recipes too bland for our group taste and lean towards the spicy side.

Most of our entrées are served in the form of one-dish meals, such as Friday Meat Loaf, Chicken Tamale Pie, or Piroshki, or a sauce served over polenta, rice, or pasta, like Orange Dijon Chicken, Hunter's Stew, or Thai Coconut Chicken. We also serve elaborate special salads and stir-frys. What you won't find at the Streamliner Diner are cuts of meat. We're not vegetarian, but we're not big meat eaters either. We have been leaning away from heavy cream and cheese dishes, but you will notice that we still have our share of rich dishes.

So hang on, and we'll share with you the kinds of interesting creations that have come out of our kitchen and pleased our customers.

Mediterranean Garden Bake

This is like eating a scrumptious hot salad. It's great on a midsummer's evening served with fresh bread and a crisp white wine.

4 8½-ounce cans artichoke
   hearts packed in water
2 cups chopped fresh Roma
   tomatoes
3 tablespoons capers
¾ cup seasoned bread crumbs
1 cup minced parsley
4 cloves garlic, minced
1 bunch green onions, chopped
1 cup grated Parmesan cheese
1 cup sliced olives
1 teaspoon salt
3 tablespoons olive oil

Preheat oven to 400°. Drain the canned artichokes and chop them finely. Put them in a large bowl along with the remaining ingredients and mix well. Divide the mixture equally between 6 individual casserole dishes. Bake at 400° for 10 to 15 minutes until the tops are golden brown.

Yield: 6 servings

Greek Pasta

■ ⸺⸺⸺⸺⸺⸺⸺⸺⸺⸺⸺⸺⸺⸺⸺⸺⸺⸺⸺ ■

This vegetarian dish bursts with flavor and color. The preparation is very easy.

    1 pound rotini
    3 cloves garlic
    1 bunch fresh basil leaves
    ¾ cup sour cream
    1¼ cups crumbled feta cheese
    pinch of pepper
    2 tablespoons olive oil
    1 bunch green onions, sliced on
         the diagonal
    1 green pepper, diced
    6 mushrooms, thickly sliced
    1 tomato, sliced into wedges
    1 cup Kalamata olives, pitted

Cook the rotini. Drain and keep warm. To prepare the sauce, blend garlic, basil, sour cream, feta cheese, and pepper in a food processor or blender. Set aside.

Heat the olive oil in a large skillet. Quickly sauté the green onions, green pepper, and mushrooms until tender-crisp. Toss with rotini and stir in the sauce. Cut the tomato wedges in half diagonally. Toss the halved tomato wedges and Kalamata olives with the rotini. Serve immediately.

Yield: 6 servings

Plenty Polenta and Marinara

This is like a deep-dish pizza with a corn crust instead of the traditional yeast dough.

Polenta (see page 227)

1½ cups sliced mushrooms
½ cup pitted Kalamata olives
½ cup ricotta cheese
½ cup chopped green pepper
2 cups Basic Italian Tomato
    Sauce (see page 228)
¼ pound grated cheddar cheese
¼ pound grated Parmesan cheese

Prepare the polenta. Let it cool until you can work it with your hands.

Preheat oven to 350°. Grease a 9×9-inch pan. Mold the polenta into the pan, building up the sides. In the polenta crust, layer the mushrooms, Kalamata olives, ricotta cheese, green pepper, tomato sauce, cheddar cheese, and Parmesan cheese in that order. Bake at 350° for 45 minutes. Remove from the oven and let sit for 10 minutes. Serve with a light green salad. This is a filling meal!

Yield: 4 servings

Stuffed Tomatoes over Polenta

Served on a bed of polenta, fresh tomatoes stuffed with Kalamata olives, pine nuts, and Parmesan cheese create a simple yet delicious meal. Try serving it with the Blue Cheese–Pear–Walnut Salad (see page 125).

Polenta (see page 227)   4 teaspoons olive oil (optional)

4 fresh tomatoes
1 cup grated Parmesan cheese
1 cup pine nuts
1 cup parsley, minced
1 cup finely chopped Kalamata
  olives
1 cup chopped green onions
1 cup seasoned bread crumbs

Prepare the polenta. Cover to keep warm while preparing the tomatoes.

Preheat oven to 375°. Grease a 9 × 13-inch baking pan. Cut the tomatoes in half horizontally and scoop out the insides into a small bowl. Let the halves sit upside down on a tray to drain. Dice 1 cup of the insides for the filling.

To prepare the filling, combine the diced tomato, Parmesan, pine nuts, parsley, olives, green onions, and bread crumbs. Make sure the ingredients are finely chopped so that the filling blends well. Toss everything together, mixing well with your hands or a large spoon.

Stuff the halved tomatoes with the filling. Drizzle olive oil over the tomatoes, if desired. Place in the baking pan and bake at 375° for 15 to 20 minutes, or just until the tops are golden brown. (You don't want the insides to be gooey.) Serve immediately on a bed of polenta.

Yield: 4 servings

Ma Po Tofu

This recipe comes from Nouri Soderland, Irene's birthday partner and Japanese teacher, who has shared her knowledge of oriental cooking with us and her many friends. Ma Po Tofu is a Chinese dish that makes use of two soybean products: tofu, which is soybean curd, and miso, which is a fermented, salted soybean paste. Both are available in the oriental food section of most large food markets. Miso will keep refrigerated indefinitely. You can substitute sugar peas or string beans for the zucchini.

2 tablespoons peanut oil or light vegetable oil

3 green onions, chopped diagonally

3 cloves garlic, minced

1 tablespoon grated fresh ginger

1½ pounds zucchini, sliced ½ inch thick

¼ cup miso

2 tablespoons brown sugar

2 tablespoons soy sauce

¼ cup catsup

dash cayenne pepper

1 12-ounce package firm tofu, drained and cubed

dash sesame oil

Brown or White Rice (see page 226)

Heat the oil in a large frying pan. Sauté the green onions, garlic, and ginger until the onions are tender. Add the zucchini, mix well, and sauté for about 10 minutes until the zucchini is barely tender.

Mix together the miso, brown sugar, soy sauce, catsup, and cayenne pepper. Add it to the cooked vegetables in the frying pan. Heat through. Add the tofu, stirring gently to coat. Drizzle in a little sesame oil, and gently toss. Remove from heat.

Serve hot over rice or serve at room temperature as a side dish. This can be refrigerated for a few days and eaten cold or reheated.

Yield: 6 to 8 servings

Irish Lasagne

Why not a layered potato, tomato, and cheese casserole? After all, potatoes can carry flavor as well as noodles. This goes well with Mushroom–Bacon–Blue Cheese Salad (see page 123).

2 large potatoes, thinly sliced
1 10-ounce package frozen spinach, or 1 bunch fresh spinach, washed
salt and pepper to taste
2 cups Basic Italian Tomato Sauce (see page 228)
1 cup Pesto, optional (see page 229)

1 15-ounce container ricotta cheese
½ pound mozzarella cheese, sliced
¼ cup grated Parmesan cheese
2 tablespoons olive oil

Preheat oven to 375°. Grease a 9×9-inch baking pan. Steam the sliced potatoes until barely tender, about 10 minutes. If using frozen spinach, cook and drain. If using fresh spinach, steam it lightly.

Layer half the potatoes in the baking pan and sprinkle with salt and pepper. Add half of the tomato sauce, all of the spinach, the optional pesto, the ricotta, and half of the mozzarella. Repeat with potatoes, salt and pepper, remaining sauce and mozzarella cheese, and all of the Parmesan cheese. Drizzle olive oil evenly over the top.

Bake covered for 30 minutes in a 375° oven. Uncover and bake until the top is bubbly and starting to brown, another 30 minutes or so.

Yield: 6 servings

Lentil Burgers

Our goal was *not* to create a substitute for hamburgers. These burgers stand on their own.

1 cup dried lentils (2½ cups cooked)

2 cups water

oil for frying

4 slices Swiss or Gruyère cheese (optional)

½ cup sunflower seeds, toasted

1 teaspoon oregano

1 teaspoon thyme

⅛ teaspoon pepper

½ teaspoon salt

1 6-ounce can tomato paste

1 onion, diced

½ cup grated carrot

2 cloves garlic, minced

2 tablespoons olive oil

2 eggs

1 cup seasoned bread crumbs

In a medium-sized saucepan, cook the lentils in 2 cups of water until they are done but firm (approximately 25 to 30 minutes). Let cool.

In a large bowl, mix cooked lentils with sunflower seeds, oregano, thyme, pepper, salt, tomato paste, onion, carrot, garlic, 2 tablespoons oil, eggs, and bread crumbs until they are the consistency of meat loaf.

Make 4 patties. Heat oil in a skillet. Fry patties on one side until browned. Flip over and, if you like, put a slice of Swiss or Gruyère cheese on each burger and let it melt. We serve each Lentil Burger on a fresh bun with Dijon mustard, lettuce, tomato, and a slice of purple onion.

Yield: 4 burgers

Pesto Monte Cristo

This delicious French toast sandwich adds a new dimension to the traditional concept of a Monte Cristo sandwich.

1 cup Pesto (see page 228)	3 eggs
6 ounces cream cheese	2 cups milk
8 slices sourdough bread	4 tablespoons butter
12 slices cooked ham	
2 thinly sliced tomatoes	

Mix the pesto with the cream cheese and spread ¼ cup of pesto-cream cheese onto each bread slice. Make 4 sandwiches with the ham and tomato slices.

In a medium-sized bowl, beat the eggs using a wire whisk and whisk in the milk. Set aside.

In a large frying pan, heat the butter over medium heat until it bubbles. Dip each sandwich into the milk and egg batter, drain off excess, and panfry as for French toast until brown on both sides. Slice on the diagonal and serve hot.

Yield: 4 servings

Eggplant Parmesan Sandwiches

With melted cheese and an aromatic tomato sauce, this fried eggplant sandwich will convert even those who are not lovers of eggplant. It is much easier to make than Eggplant Parmesan.

1 eggplant (1½ pounds)	2 cups Basic Italian Tomato
2 teaspoons salt	Sauce (see page 228)
	4 slices sourdough bread
2 eggs	½ cup olive oil
¼ cup water	2 cups grated mozzarella cheese
¾ cup unbleached white flour	(½ pound)
1 cup Italian-style bread crumbs	½ cup grated Parmesan cheese

Cut the eggplant into ½-inch slices. There will be about 12 slices. Lightly salt the slices and place them in a bowl. Let sit for 30 minutes. Drain and pat dry.

Beat the eggs and water together. Dip the eggplant into flour, shake off the excess, dip it into the eggs, and finally in the bread crumbs, coating it on both sides. If you are preparing the dish in advance, refrigerate it at this point.

For the final preparation, heat the tomato sauce in a small saucepan. Toast the bread slices and arrange them on a cookie sheet. Heat 2 tablespoons of olive oil in a large frying pan. Fry the breaded eggplant slices, 3 or 4 at a time, for 2 minutes on each side or until nicely browned on the outside, and soft when pierced with a fork. Remove the fried eggplant and slide it onto the toast. Add more oil and continue frying until all the eggplant slices are cooked and mounded up on the bread.

Preheat the broiler to 500°. Top each sandwich with ½ cup hot tomato sauce, ½ cup mozzarella, and 2 tablespoons Parmesan. Broil for 2 to 3 minutes, or until the cheese is hot and bubbly. Serve immediately. Caesar Salad (see page 130) makes a nice accompaniment.

Yield: 4 sandwiches

Tofu Reubens

Tofu Reuben may seem oxymoronic, in a culinary sense, but really, these sandwiches are incredibly delicious. Try them!

5 cloves garlic, minced	12 slices dill rye or dark rye
1 cup soy sauce	bread
1 cup rice vinegar	mustard
2 teaspoons salt	6 slices tomato
1 teaspoon pepper	16 ounces sauerkraut
¼ cup honey	
1 tablespoon grated fresh ginger	
16 ounces firm tofu, drained	
6 slices Swiss cheese or Gruyère cheese	

In a medium-sized bowl, mix the garlic, soy sauce, vinegar, salt, pepper, honey, and ginger with a wire whisk until well blended. Slice the tofu into 6 thin rectangles. Marinate them in the soy sauce and vinegar mixture for at least 2 hours. You can marinate them overnight as well.

In a heavy skillet or frying pan, brown the tofu on one side. Flip over and put one slice of cheese on top. Cover and let melt.

Toast the rye bread, put mustard on the toast, then flip the tofu onto the toast. Top with tomato slices and sauerkraut, and voilà!

Note: The marinade can be saved. It makes a great sweet-and-sour sauce (thicken it with cornstarch) for shrimp fried rice. It can also be used as a stock for soup, such as Vegetarian Onion, or Egg–Onion–Tarragon Soup (see pages 95 and 97). Don't throw it away!

Yield: 6 sandwiches

Fried Cheese with Green Apples and Horseradish Sauce

We serve this as a light summer lunch, but it would be a delectable appetizer. Just cut the cheese into smaller pieces.

1 tablespoon butter	2 tart green apples
1 tablespoon unbleached white flour	juice of 1 lemon
1/2 cup milk	1 pound mozzarella cheese
1 teaspoon prepared horseradish	1/3 cup unbleached white flour
1/2 teaspoon Dijon mustard	1 egg
1/2 teaspoon sugar	1 tablespoon water
1 teaspoon vinegar	1/2 cup seasoned bread crumbs
pinch salt	4 tablespoons light oil for frying
pinch pepper	

In a small saucepan, heat the butter until it bubbles. Add 1 tablespoon flour and stir to make a paste. Continue to cook over a medium heat, stirring until the flour starts to turn golden. Add the milk in a steady stream, whisking briskly. Cook, stirring continually, until the sauce is smooth and thick. Add the horseradish, mustard, sugar, vinegar, salt, and pepper. Mix well. Adjust the flavors to your liking. If the sauce needs thinning, just add milk. Turn heat to low, stirring occasionally to avoid scorching.

Slice the apples into rings using 1/2 apple for each serving. Squeeze lemon juice over the apples to keep them from browning. Set aside.

Cut the mozzarella into 4 slices, each 1/2 inch thick. Put 1/3 cup of flour in a shallow dish (to flour the cheese). Beat the egg with the water in a second dish. Put the bread crumbs in a third dish. Dip the cheese in the flour to coat, then the egg wash, and then the bread crumbs.

For each cheese cutlet, heat 1 tablespoon of oil in a frying pan. Brown the cheese on one side. Flip over and brown on the other side. Test with a fork to make sure that cheese has melted all the way through. There should not be any resistance from the cheese. This usually takes 3 to 4 minutes. Slide onto a plate and serve at once with the horseradish sauce and apples.

Yield: 4 servings

Butternut Tarts

These petite autumn harvest pies are luscious. They are wonderful as a side dish or as a main dish for a vegetarian meal.

1 butternut squash (2 cups mashed)

8 ounces cream cheese
½ cup half-and-half
2 eggs, beaten
2 tablespoons honey
1 teaspoon salt
1 teaspoon cinnamon
½ teaspoon allspice
¼ teaspoon nutmeg
zest of 1 orange, minced

2 recipes Pie Crust, unbaked (see page 219)
½ cup Herbed Garlic Crouton crumbs (see page 133), or
½ cup toasted almonds, finely chopped

Peel and cube the squash. Steam it until it is very tender, about 30 minutes. Mash.

Using an electric mixer, whip together the cream cheese, half-and-half, eggs, honey, salt, cinnamon, allspice, nutmeg, and orange zest. Whip in the mashed squash until light and fluffy.

Roll out the pie dough and cut rounds to fit the tart pans. Line the pans with the dough and crimp the edges. Fill the shells with the squash mixture. Top each tart with bread crumbs or toasted almonds.

Bake 20 to 30 minutes at 350° until the pie crusts are golden and a knife inserted in the squash comes out clean.

Yield: Six to eight 4-inch tarts

Artichoke Heart–Brie Turnovers

The flavor of these savory turnovers might remind you of that mysterious hot artichoke dip that's called "What's In This?" These can be made ahead of time and refrigerated until guests arrive. Pop them into the oven for about 35 minutes and serve as an appetizer or as part of the main meal. They are unforgettable. We use artichoke hearts canned in water, not marinated artichokes.

1 recipe Pie Crust, unbaked
   (see page 219)

1 egg
1 tablespoon water

¼ pound Brie cheese
1 8½-ounce can artichoke
   hearts, well drained
2 tablespoons grated Parmesan
   cheese
1 cup ricotta cheese
1 tablespoon capers

Prepare the pie dough. Refrigerate until ready to use.

Cut the Brie into ¼-inch chunks. Coarsely chop the artichoke hearts. Combine the Brie, artichoke hearts, Parmesan, ricotta, and capers.

Divide the pie dough into 4 equal parts. Form each into a ball and flatten. With a rolling pin, roll each one into an 8-inch round. Divide the filling equally among the dough rounds, placing the filling on half of each round. Fold the other half over the filling and crimp the edges. Prick the tops with a fork.

Beat the egg with water. Brush the tops of the turnovers with the egg wash. Bake at 375° for 35 minutes or until the outside is brown and the inside is bubbly.

Yield: 4 turnovers

Piroshki

Piroshki are as popular in Russia as hamburgers are in the U.S.A. If you can't make pie dough, cheat and buy some ready-to-bake biscuit dough. Roll out the dough, fill it, and bake as directed in the recipe. Piroshki can be made ahead and frozen before baking. They can be eaten hot or cold: cold ones are great for picnics.

1 recipe Pie Crust, unbaked (see page 219), or 1 tube biscuit dough	1 egg 1 tablespoon water

½ pound ground beef
½ cup diced onion
1 hard-boiled egg, chopped
2 tablespoons mayonnaise
1 teaspoon dried dill weed
½ teaspoon salt
½ teaspoon pepper

Prepare pie dough and set aside.

In a large frying pan, brown the ground beef. Add the onion and cook until transparent. Remove from heat and add the egg, mayonnaise, dill, salt, and pepper. Mix until all is incorporated. Set aside.

Preheat oven to 375°. On a lightly floured surface, divide pie dough into 4 equal parts. Form each into a ball and flatten. Roll each one out into an 8-inch round. Divide the filling equally among the dough rounds, placing it on half of each round. Fold the other half over the filling and crimp the edges. Prick the tops with a fork to let steam escape.

Beat the egg with water and brush the tops of the piroshki with egg wash. Place piroshki, a few inches apart, on a greased baking sheet. Bake at 375° for 35 minutes or until brown.

Yield: 4 piroshki

Spinach–Pine Nut Calzone

You don't have to be Italian to enjoy this dish. If you are not serving a large number of people, these are great the next day.

1 cup warm water

1 tablespoon active dry yeast

1 tablespoon honey

2 eggs

¼ cup olive oil

1½ teaspoons salt

1 cup chopped pine nuts, toasted

4 to 5 cups unbleached white
    flour

1 cup ricotta cheese

¾ cup grated Parmesan cheese

¼ teaspoon pepper

½ teaspoon salt

1 egg

1 egg, beaten

1 tablespoon butter

1 onion, diced

4 cloves garlic, minced

2 cups sliced mushrooms

1 bunch spinach, washed and
    stemmed

Mix warm water, yeast, and honey in a large bowl. Set it aside until it begins to bubble. With a wire whisk, beat in 2 eggs, oil, and 1½ teaspoons salt. Whisk in the pine nuts.

With a large mixing spoon, stir in the flour, 1 cup at a time, until the dough becomes too stiff to stir. Turn the dough out onto your work area and knead in the rest of the flour, a little at a time, until the dough is smooth and elastic. It should grab the work surface and let go. Clean and oil the mixing bowl. Place the dough in the bowl. Cover and let rise to double in size in a warm, draft-free place. This will take approximately 30 minutes.

To make the filling, heat the butter in a large skillet or frying pan. Sauté the onion and garlic until the onion becomes transparent. Add the mushrooms and spinach. Sauté another 3 minutes until the spinach wilts and the mushrooms are tender.

In a large mixing bowl, combine the ricotta and Parmesan cheeses, pepper, salt, and 1 egg until well blended. Add the sautéed vegetables and mix thoroughly.

Preheat oven to 350°. Grease two 11 × 17-inch baking sheets. Turn the dough out onto a lightly floured surface. Divide it into 7 or 8 equal pieces. Form each piece into a ball and flatten with your hand. With a rolling pin, roll each piece into ⅛-inch-thick rounds. Divide the filling equally among the dough rounds. Place filling onto half of each round, fold the other half over it, and crimp the edges. Prick the tops with a fork.

Brush the tops with the beaten egg. Place 3 or 4 calzones on each baking sheet. Bake at 350° for 20 minutes, or until the tops of the calzones are golden brown. Remove from oven and let cool 5 to 10 minutes before serving.

Yield: 7 or 8 calzones

Onion Bacon Tart

In the form of a deep-dish pizza, this tart is suitable for brunch, lunch, or dinner. The savory flavors of onion, Dijon mustard, bacon, and caraway will make your taste buds blossom. Any leftovers can be reheated.

1 tablespoon active dry yeast	4 slices bacon
2 tablespoons lukewarm water	5 large onions, thinly sliced
2 teaspoons sugar	4 tablespoons bacon fat or butter
	2 eggs, beaten
1 cup milk	½ cup yogurt or sour cream
½ cup butter	1 tablespoon caraway seeds
1½ teaspoons salt	½ cup Dijon mustard
3 cups unbleached white flour	

In a large bowl, dissolve the yeast in water and add the sugar. Let sit for 5 minutes until bubbly.

Scald the milk and pour it over the butter and salt. This melts the butter and cools the milk slightly. When lukewarm, add it to the yeast mixture.

Beat in the flour, a little at a time, until the dough is stiff enough to knead. Turn onto a lightly floured surface and knead in the rest of the flour until the dough is smooth. Place the dough in a greased bowl. Cover with plastic wrap and put in a warm, draft-free place. Let rise until double in bulk, about 1 hour.

In a large skillet, fry the bacon until crisp. Remove the bacon and crumble it. Pour off all but 4 tablespoons of bacon fat.

Sauté the onions slowly in the fat or in 4 tablespoons of butter, if you prefer, until tender. This may take up to 20 minutes. Cool slightly.

Mix together the eggs, yogurt or sour cream, caraway seeds, cooked bacon, and the onion. Set aside.

When dough has risen, preheat the oven to 375° and grease a 10 × 15-inch baking pan. Punch down the dough and roll it out to fit the baking pan. Place the dough in the pan, building up the sides, pizza fashion. Spread mustard over this up to ½ inch from the edge. Then top with the onion mixture.

Bake at 375° for about 35 minutes. Cut into squares. For a light dinner or great luncheon, serve with a green salad or a cup of soup.

Yield: 8 servings

VARIATION

Substitute anchovies and olives for the bacon and caraway seeds.

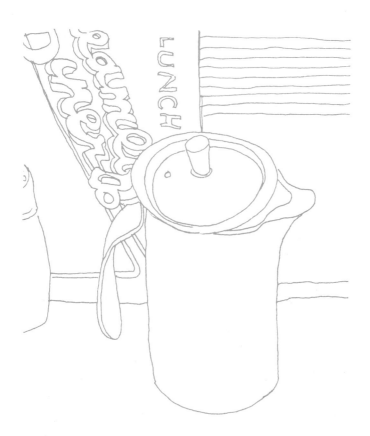

Fillo Rustica

We love to experiment with delicate fillo pastry leaves. They add elegance and a textural dimension to a dish. In this dish, we take a Torte Rustica and substitute fillo pastry for the usual brioche dough, building up layers in a baclava format. This recipe makes beautiful hors d'oeuvres that taste like antipasto in pastry. This dish can be prepared a day ahead of time. If there are leftovers, it is good cold and also reheats well.

1 tablespoon olive oil
1 onion, diced
1 green pepper, diced
4 cloves garlic, minced
½ teaspoon oregano
¼ teaspoon thyme
½ teaspoon salt
¼ teaspoon pepper

1 6-ounce jar Italian-style
   roasted peppers
1 8½-ounce can artichoke hearts
4 ounces Italian or Greek olives
¼ teaspoon salt
1 15-ounce container ricotta
   cheese

1 1-pound package fillo leaves
6 tablespoons butter, melted
4 ounces thinly sliced prosciutto
   or ham
4 ounces thinly sliced hard Italian
   salami
4 ounces shredded Parmesan
   cheese

Heat the olive oil in a medium-sized skillet. Sauté the onion, green pepper, garlic, oregano, thyme, ½ teaspoon salt, and pepper until the onion is transparent, about 5 minutes. Set aside.

Drain and chop the roasted peppers and artichoke hearts. Pit and chop the olives. In a medium-sized bowl mix together the roasted peppers, artichoke hearts, olives, ¼ teaspoon salt, and half of the ricotta. Set aside.

Grease a 9 × 13-inch baking pan. Unroll the fillo from the package. Cut the stack in half widthwise so that they fit the pan. Put one stack on top of the other and cover with plastic wrap or a damp towel and keep covered as you are working with it. Fillo dries out very quickly.

Lay 1 fillo sheet in the baking pan. Using your fingers or a pastry brush, spread butter as sparingly as possible over the entire sheet. Using too much butter makes it greasy. Repeat the process 5 more times until you have a stack of 6 buttered fillo leaves. Don't panic if you tear the fillo. The final sheet is the only one that will be seen. Put a layer of prosciutto or ham and the remaining ricotta over the 6th sheet of fillo.

Continue the layering process with 6 sheets of buttered fillo, pepper-onion mixture, 6 sheets of buttered fillo, salami and half the Parmesan, more fillo, then the artichoke mixture topped by the rest of the Parmesan, and finally a layer of 9 buttered fillo leaves. Wrap the leftover fillo in plastic; it will keep refrigerated for 5 weeks.

Cut the Fillo Rustica into 6 or 24 squares. Be sure to cut all the way to the bottom of the pan. The pastry is very flaky once baked and difficult to cut.

Bake uncovered in a preheated 375° oven for 40 to 45 minutes until the fillo is golden brown and crisp on top. Serve with a Caesar Salad (see page 130) for a delightful meal.

Yield: 6 servings or 24 hors d'oeuvres

Chicken Dijon Fillo Rolls

In this dish the layers of buttered fillo leaves are filled with poultry, vegetables, and seasonings, then rolled up and baked.

3 pounds chicken parts	1 1-pound package fillo leaves
2 cups finely chopped green onions	¾ cup butter, melted
1 cup sliced black olives	1 bunch spinach leaves, washed
½ cup Dijon mustard	
zest of 1 orange, minced	
1 teaspoon salt	
1 teaspoon pepper	

In a 3-quart saucepan bring the chicken parts to a boil in water to cover. Lower heat and simmer until tender, about 20 minutes. Remove the chicken. When cool enough to handle, remove the meat from the bones and cut into bite-sized pieces. Refrigerate the broth and save for another use.

In a medium-sized bowl, mix together the chicken, green onions, olives, mustard, orange zest, salt, and pepper.

Unroll the fillo from the package. Cover with plastic wrap or a damp towel and keep covered as you are working with it. Fillo dries out very quickly. Lay a sheet of fillo out on a dry surface or on waxed paper. Using either your finger-tips or a pastry brush, spread a thin wash of melted butter as sparingly as possible across the entire surface of the fillo. Using too much butter will make it greasy. Lay another sheet of fillo on top of the first one. Repeat the process until you have 6 sheets of buttered fillo. Now make two more stacks of fillo just like the first one.

On each stack of fillo arrange a row of overlapping spinach leaves lengthwise down the middle. Lay ⅓ of the chicken mixture in a line down the center of the spinach. Roll each rectangle into a long roll. Place in a greased baking pan and cut each roll into 6 sections. Brush the tops with butter. Bake at 350° for 35 to 45 minutes or until the fillo is golden.

Yield: 4 to 6 servings

VARIATION

Substitute 2 teaspoons tarragon for the orange zest.

Southern Fried Chicken

This chicken is good hot or cold. For the perfect picnic, pack up some cold Southern Fried Chicken and a batch of Grandma's Potato Salad (see page 119).

1 3½-pound frying chicken	2 eggs, slightly beaten
3 cups unbleached white flour	¾ cup milk
2 teaspoons salt	4 cups vegetable oil
2 teaspoons pepper	
1 tablespoon fresh rosemary, finely chopped (optional)	

Cut the chicken into serving pieces. Using two paper bags, one inside the other, combine the flour, salt, pepper, and optional rosemary.

Mix the eggs and milk in a bowl suitable for dipping the chicken. In a 12-inch frying pan, heat the oil until hot, but not smoking. Meanwhile, bread the chicken pieces, a few at a time, by dipping them into the egg mixture, draining off excess liquid, and then dropping them into the bag of flour. Shake to coat the chicken.

Add half of the chicken to the hot oil, skin side down; don't crowd the pan. Cook on one side until brown, about 10 minutes, then turn and brown the other side, for another 10 minutes. Turn once again and fry for 5 more minutes. Poke with a fork to test for doneness. Chicken juices should run clear with no pink. Each batch takes about 25 minutes. Remove pieces to paper towels and keep warm in the oven while frying the remainder of the chicken.

Note: The oil can be reused for frying once more if it is strained to remove breading particles. The seasoned flour can also be reused for breading if it is sifted and refrigerated in an airtight plastic container.

Yield: 4 servings

Dad's Chicken Pot Pie

Alexandra's father has lived in West Germany for twenty-five years. Naturally, he misses some of his old American favorites, so this recipe was his special request and is dedicated to him. The following rendition is a little unusual in that there is a biscuit layer on top. If you prefer a pot pie that looks like a pie, double the Pie Crust recipe (see page 219) instead of using biscuits. Spoon the filling into an unbaked pie shell, top with the crust, crimp, and bake at 350° until the pie crust is golden brown, about 45 minutes.

2 pounds chicken parts
1 potato, diced
1 tablespoon butter
1 onion, diced
1 carrot, diced
1 cup fresh or frozen peas
1 cup fresh or frozen whole kernel
   corn
1 recipe Basil Cream Sauce (see
   page 64), reducing milk to 3
   cups

2 cups unbleached white flour
1 tablespoon baking powder
¾ teaspoon salt
½ cup margarine
1 cup milk

In a 3-quart pot, bring the chicken parts to a boil in water to cover. Lower heat and simmer until tender, about 20 minutes. Strain and reserve the liquid. Remove the bones and chop the meat into bite-sized pieces. Set aside.

Boil or steam the potatoes until just tender, about 15 minutes. Melt the butter in a medium-sized skillet. Add the onion and sauté until transparent. Add the carrot and sauté for another 2 minutes. Add the peas and corn. Remove from heat.

Prepare the Basil Cream Sauce with 3 cups of milk. In a large bowl, thoroughly mix together the sauce with the potatoes, vegetables, and chicken. Pour the mixture into an 8×8-inch baking pan. Bake at 350° for 20 minutes to heat through. Meanwhile, get the drop biscuits ready.

To make the biscuits, mix together the flour, baking powder, and salt in a medium-sized bowl. Cut in the margarine with two knives or a pastry cutter until it is all a large, even crumb. Gently stir in the milk, taking care not to overmix.

Remove the pan from oven after 20 minutes and drop biscuit batter from a large spoon to make rows of biscuits across the top of the chicken-vegetable mixture. Bake for an additional 20 minutes or until the biscuits are done and beginning to brown on top.

Yield: 4 servings

VARIATION

Substitute a handful of minced fresh tarragon or two teaspoons of dried tarragon for the basil in the Basil Cream Sauce recipe.

Orange Dijon Chicken

The fresh, zesty flavor of orange combines well with mustard as a marinade for baked chicken. Serve this dish with a bowl of hot rice to soak up the wonderful sauce.

juice and zest of 2 oranges
juice and zest of 1 lemon
4 tablespoons Dijon mustard
⅓ cup brown sugar, packed
3 tablespoons butter, melted
2 pounds boneless chicken, cubed

Brown or White Rice (see
   page 226)
2 carrots, sliced
1 teaspoon salt

In a small bowl, mix together the orange and lemon zest and juice, mustard, sugar, and melted butter. Pour it over the chicken in a medium-sized casserole dish, and marinate for a few hours, or overnight for greater flavor.

Preheat oven to 375° and bake in covered casserole dish for 50 minutes. Stir occasionally.

While the chicken is baking, prepare the rice. It should be finished cooking about the same time the chicken is ready to serve. After the chicken has cooked for 30 minutes, steam the carrots in a small saucepan with ¼ cup water and 1 teaspoon salt for a few minutes until just tender. Drain and mix the carrots with the chicken. Continue to bake for another 15 minutes or until the chicken is very tender. Serve hot over rice.

Yield: 4 to 6 servings

Chicken Tamale Pie

This Tex-Mex dish is simple to prepare and certain to appease the appetites of both children and adults.

2 pounds chicken parts
5 cups water

3 cups grated cheddar cheese
  (¾ pound)
1 cup fresh or frozen whole kernel
  corn
2 4-ounce cans chopped green
  chilies
1 2¼-ounce can sliced black
  olives, drained
1 onion, diced
¾ cup Streamliner Salsa (see
  page 230)
2 teaspoons cumin
1 teaspoon salt

4 cups chicken stock
1 teaspoon salt
2 cups cornmeal

In a 3-quart pot, bring the chicken to a boil in 5 cups of water. Lower the heat and simmer until tender, about 20 minutes. Strain and reserve the liquid. Remove the bones and cut the chicken into bite-sized pieces. Set aside.

In a large bowl, mix together 1 cup grated cheese, corn, 1 can of chilies, black olives, onion, salsa, cumin, and 1 teaspoon of salt.

Bring 4 cups of the reserved chicken stock and 1 teaspoon of salt to a boil in the same 3-quart pot. Slowly stir in the cornmeal with a wire whisk. Lower heat and stir frequently until it is the consistency of a thick mush, about 5 minutes. Stir in the second can of chilies and 1 cup cheddar cheese. Remove from the heat and allow to cool slightly.

Grease a 12-inch round deep-dish baking pan. (Cast-iron skillets work well.) When cool enough to handle, spread the mush over the bottom of the pan and build up the sides. Spoon the chicken-vegetable mixture into the mush shell and top with the remaining cheese.

Bake at 350° for 35 to 45 minutes until heated through. If you would like further embellishments, you can serve the tamale pie topped with sour cream and offer Guacamole (see page 232) and Streamliner Salsa with jalapeños (see page 230) for those who like it hot.

Yield: 4 servings

Hunter's Stew

When the chanterelles are calling from under the huckleberries and the leaves are turning, it is time for Hunter's Stew. Irene, our resident mushroom expert, has created this savory dish of chicken, wine, chanterelles, and tomato. Commercially grown mushrooms can be substituted, but the wild ingredient is well worth the hunt. We serve the stew with polenta.

1 3-pound chicken, cut into serving-sized pieces
1 cup unbleached white flour
4 tablespoons butter
2 tablespoons olive oil
2 cups sliced mushrooms, domestic or wild
½ cup dry red wine

½ cup chicken stock or water
1 cup tomato juice or tomato sauce
½ teaspoon salt
½ teaspoon pepper

Polenta (see page 227)

2 large carrots, diced
1 cup fresh or frozen peas

Roll the chicken pieces in flour. Brown the chicken in the butter and olive oil over medium heat in a large cast-iron pan or heavy-bottomed 4-quart pot. This chicken browning process will have to be done in two batches. Remove the chicken and set aside.

Add the mushrooms to the drippings and sauté until tender. Add the wine and cook over high heat until the liquid is reduced by half. Reduce the heat.

Add stock or water, tomato juice or tomato sauce, chicken, salt, and pepper. Cover and cook for 30 minutes.

Meanwhile, prepare the polenta and set it aside.

Add the carrots to the chicken and cook for another 15 minutes. Add the peas and cook for another 5 minutes or until carrots are tender. Serve over the polenta with generous amounts of sauce.

Yield: 4 to 6 servings

Thai Coconut Chicken

Once when Irene was experimenting with different combinations of herbs and spices, she ground together some cumin seed, anise seed, and peppercorns and used them to season a breading for chicken. The dish that resulted is reminiscent of a Thai coconut chicken dish.

1 cup water
2 large ancho chilies
2 tablespoons cumin seed
1½ tablespoons anise seed
1½ teaspoons black peppercorns
1½ tablespoons cinnamon
½ cup unbleached white flour

3 pounds chicken, cut into
   serving-sized pieces
½ cup light cooking oil
1 14-ounce can coconut milk
1 sweet red pepper, cut into strips
1 stalk lemon grass
2 tablespoons mirin (sweet rice
   cooking wine)

juice of 1 lime
1 teaspoon salt, or to taste
3 tablespoons honey

Brown or White Rice (see
   page 226)

Bring water to boil in a frying pan with a lid. Drop in the chilies and simmer for 10 minutes. Remove and cool. Remove seeds and scrape the flesh from chilies. Add the chili flesh back into the water in the pan and reserve.

Meanwhile grind the cumin seed, anise seed, and whole black pepper with a mortar and pestle. Add the cinnamon and flour to the spices after they are ground. Mix well. Put the flour in a shallow bowl and dredge the chicken pieces in the seasoned flour.

Heat the oil in a large cast-iron skillet. Brown the chicken pieces on both sides, not crowding the pan, until all pieces are browned. This takes about 20 minutes. Remove the chicken, drain all but 2 tablespoons of pan drippings, and return the chicken to the pot. Add the liquid and pulp from the ancho chilies, coconut milk, red pepper strips, lemon grass, and rice wine. Cover with a lid and turn heat down to medium low. Simmer for 1 hour.

Just before serving, add the lime juice, salt, and honey. Serve with brown or white rice.

Yield: 4 to 6 servings

Chicken Liver Spiedini

Even folks who don't like chicken liver acquire a taste for this grilled delicacy.

1 pound chicken livers	1/2 loaf day-old French bread
1 tablespoon vinegar	1 small bunch sage leaves
2 tablespoons butter	8 skewers

1/2 pound whole mushrooms,
   halved if extra large
2 tablespoons butter
2 tablespoons soy sauce
1 tablespoon dry cooking sherry

Soak the livers in vinegar and water to cover for 30 minutes. Drain and pat dry. Cut the livers apart and remove any membranes. Panfry in 2 tablespoons of butter quickly, until browned. Don't overcook. Remove livers from the pan and reserve the juice.

Wash and drain the mushrooms. In a small saucepan, melt 2 tablespoons of butter. Add the soy sauce, sherry, and mushrooms, stirring to coat the mushrooms. Cover and cook until the liquid reaches a full boil. Turn off the heat. Drain off the liquid into the reserved juice from the liver.

Cut the bread into 1½-inch cubes. Alternately skewer mushrooms, liver, and bread, dipping the bread into the liquid before skewering. Add a few sage leaves to each skewer. Begin and end with a mushroom. Brush any remaining juice onto the skewers and broil until the bread cubes are browned, about 10 minutes. Turn once during cooking.

Note: These skewers are also wonderful barbecued.

Yield: 4 servings

Enchilada Mole

This recipe was a sworn secret for twenty years, until Irene's friend Karen Le Quey, a restaurant owner herself and the keeper of this recipe, finally decided to let the mole out of the bag. The proportions have changed from a four-gallon quantity down to a manageable five servings. This is a very filling dish and is delicious served with a green salad tossed with our Basil–Lime–Avocado Dressing (see page 132) and a good Mexican beer. Mysterious flavors permeate the mole sauce. For the best results, use Mexican chocolate: it's made with a special combination of sugar, cacao, almonds, cinnamon, and lecithin. These enchiladas can be prepared ahead of time and refrigerated.

$\frac{1}{2}$ cup oil

$3\frac{1}{2}$ teaspoons unbleached white flour

$2\frac{1}{2}$ teaspoons chili powder

3 cups water or chicken stock (or use 1 teaspoon chicken base with 3 cups water)

$\frac{1}{2}$ teaspoon ground cloves

$\frac{1}{2}$ teaspoon cinnamon

2 tablespoons cumin

1 round Mexican chocolate (3 ounces), grated

$1\frac{1}{2}$ pounds ground beef

2 cups diced onion

2 cloves garlic, minced

1 14-ounce can whole tomatoes

2 teaspoons oregano

1 tablespoon cumin

2 tablespoons prepared mustard

1 tablespoon salt

1 teaspoon pepper

$\frac{1}{4}$ cup oil

10 flour tortillas

4 cups grated cheddar cheese

$1\frac{1}{4}$ cups green onions, chopped

1 cup sour cream

$1\frac{1}{2}$ cups black olives, sliced

Streamliner Salsa (see page 230)

Heat oil in a 3- to 4-quart heavy-bottomed pan. Mix the flour and chili powder together. Add it to the oil and cook, stirring frequently until it starts to darken. Be careful not to burn it. Remove from heat. Add the water or chicken stock and stir briskly to avoid lumps.

In a small bowl, mix together the cloves, cinnamon, and 2 tablespoons cumin with the chocolate and add it to the sauce. Cook for 2 to 3 hours over low heat, stirring occasionally. The sauce will thicken and become velvety.

Meanwhile, sauté the ground beef until the pink color is gone. Add the diced onion and garlic and cook until the onion is transparent. Add the tomatoes, oregano, 1 tablespoon cumin, mustard, salt, and pepper. Cook for 15 minutes to combine the flavors.

Grease a 9 × 13-inch baking pan. Heat a little oil in a frying pan. Dip the tortillas in hot oil a few minutes on each side to soften them. Then dip each one in a little bit of the sauce and fill with ½ cup of the ground meat, ¼ cup grated cheese, and 2 tablespoons chopped green onions. Roll each filled tortilla and place it in the baking pan. Pour the remaining sauce over the rolled tortillas and top with the remaining grated cheese. At this point the dish can be refrigerated until ready to bake.

Bake in a 350° oven until bubbly, approximately 1 hour. Serve topped with sour cream, olives, and a side of salsa.

Yield: 5 servings

Friday Meat Loaf

Friday is often our busiest day for lunch. Many island carpenters come in expecting a hefty meal, and meat loaf fills the bill. We serve it hot, smothered in the Basic Italian Tomato Sauce (see page 228), or as a cold sandwich.

4 slices bread
1 cup milk

1½ pounds ground beef
1 onion, diced
2 eggs, slightly beaten
½ cup catsup
1 teaspoon Worcestershire sauce
1½ teaspoons salt
1 teaspoon pepper
4 eggs, hard-boiled and peeled (optional)

Tear up the bread and put it into a bowl along with the milk and let it sit for a few minutes until the milk has been absorbed. Mash up the bread with your fingers.

In another bowl, combine the ground beef with the onion, beaten eggs, catsup, Worcestershire sauce, salt, and pepper. Add the soaked bread and mix thoroughly.

Place the meat in a 9 × 12 × 3-inch baking pan, and smooth the top to form a solid loaf. If you are adding eggs, make a slot down the middle of the loaf, put the eggs in the slot, and smooth the meat loaf up and over the eggs.

Cover with foil and bake at 350° for 1 hour. Remove foil and continue to bake for another 30 minutes.

Yield: 6 to 8 servings

Coastal Shrimp and Crab Gumbo

The idea for this recipe came from Houston, where those wonderful Gulf Coast shrimp are plentiful. Any medium-sized or larger shrimp will work. Gumbo reheats and freezes very well. If you prefer to use chicken stock instead of making your own shrimp stock, reduce the salt.

1/2 pound fresh or frozen
  medium-sized shrimp
1 1/2 cups water

1/4 cup olive oil
1/2 cup unbleached white flour
1/2 green pepper, diced
1 onion, diced
4 cloves garlic, minced
1 10-ounce package frozen sliced
  okra, or 1 1/4 cups fresh
1 14 1/2-ounce can stewed
  tomatoes

1/2 teaspoon ground coriander
  seed
1/2 teaspoon thyme
1/8 teaspoon ground cloves
1/8 teaspoon ground allspice
1 1/2 teaspoons salt
2 teaspoons Tabasco sauce
1 bay leaf
pinch cayenne pepper

White Rice (see page 226)
1/2 pound crabmeat

To make a shrimp stock, peel the shrimp and put the peels and tails into a 2-quart pot. (Refrigerate shrimp meat until ready to use.) Add 1 1/2 cups of water and bring it to a simmer. Cook slowly over low heat for 20 minutes or longer. When ready to use stock, strain to remove the skins and tails.

To make the roux, heat the olive oil in a small, heavy-bottomed saucepan. Sprinkle the flour onto the oil and start stirring with a whisk. Stir constantly until the roux turns very brown, the color of a caramel. Add the green pepper, onion, and garlic to the roux and cook for a few minutes. Add the okra and cook a few more minutes until the okra gets stringy. Add the vegetables to the stock, including the tomatoes.

Add the coriander, thyme, cloves, allspice, salt, Tabasco sauce, bay leaf, and cayenne. Cover and cook slowly over low heat for 45 minutes.

Meanwhile, prepare the rice and keep it hot.

Add the shrimp and crab to the vegetables and continue cooking for another 15 to 20 minutes. Adjust seasonings. Serve over rice. This is especially good a day later when the spices have had a chance to mingle.

Yield: 4 servings

excellent!

Italian Poached Fish

If you ever get tired of grilling or broiling fish, throw some citrus, herbs, and onions in a skillet together with a little wine and tomatoes and poach a fish. This is lovely with a firm white fish such as cod or halibut, but we have also used marlin, sea bass, and salmon, depending on what is available. A generous portion is about ½ pound per person.

3 tablespoons olive oil

4 cloves garlic, minced

1 onion, diced

6 Roma tomatoes, chopped
   (1 pound)

1 tablespoon grated orange zest

1 tablespoon anise seed

1 cup chopped fresh basil

1 cup red wine

2 tablespoons honey

½ teaspoon pepper

¾ teaspoon salt

1½ to 2 pounds Alaskan cod or
   halibut fillets

Heat the oil in a large skillet. Sauté the garlic, onion, and tomatoes on high heat until the onion is transparent and the tomatoes are releasing their juices. Add the orange zest, anise seed, basil, red wine, honey, pepper, and salt. Continue cooking on high heat until the wine and juices are boiling. Lower heat and simmer for 10 to 15 minutes.

Cut the fish into serving-sized pieces. Lay the pieces on top of the sauce in the skillet. Cover and continue simmering for 5 to 10 minutes, or until the fish flakes apart. Serve the fish with the sauce spooned over it.

Yield: 4 servings

Shrimp Egg Rolls

These egg rolls are filled with shrimp, vegetables, and bean sprouts, then deep fried and dipped in a Chinese sweet-and-sour sauce. They are crunchy, chewy, and satisfying.

3 tablespoons peanut oil or other light vegetable oil

4 cups shredded green cabbage

1 onion, diced

1 stalk celery, diced

1 carrot, grated

1 green onion, chopped

1 cup mung bean sprouts

1½ teaspoons grated fresh ginger

1 clove garlic, minced

4 ounces small shrimp

¼ cup fresh or frozen peas

¼ cup mirin (sweet rice cooking wine)

2 tablespoons cornstarch

¼ cup water

1½ tablespoons soy sauce

dash sesame oil

1 package egg roll wrappers

light oil for deep frying (enough to cover egg rolls in pot)

Sweet-and-Sour Sauce (see page 178)

In a large frying pan or wok, heat the oil over high heat. Add the cabbage, onion, celery, carrot, and green onion. Sauté briefly until the vegetables are limp, stirring frequently. Add the bean sprouts, ginger, garlic, shrimp, and peas. Cook all until heated through. Add the mirin.

Mix the cornstarch with water and soy sauce. Add to the wok and cook, stirring constantly until the sauce thickens and clears. Remove from heat. Add sesame oil and allow to cool slightly.

Using an ice cream scoop, place 1 scoop of filling in the center of the egg roll wrapper. Fold it up envelope style, first from the bottom up, then over from both sides. Moisten the top edge with water and fold it down to seal.

In a heavy-bottomed pot or frying pan, fry the egg rolls seam side down in hot oil, a few at a time. Don't let the oil smoke and don't crowd the pan. Turn and brown on the other side. Watch them carefully as they cook quickly. Remove and drain on paper towels. Keep the egg rolls warm in the oven until ready to serve. Serve with Sweet-and-Sour Sauce.

Yield: 14 egg rolls

Sweet-and-Sour Sauce

¼ cup pineapple juice

1½ tablespoons vegetable oil

3 tablespoons brown sugar, packed

1½ teaspoons soy sauce

¼ teaspoon pepper

2 tablespoons vinegar

2 tablespoons catsup

¼ onion, grated

1 tablespoon cornstarch

1 tablespoon cold water

Combine the pineapple juice, oil, brown sugar, soy sauce, pepper, vinegar, catsup, and onion. Cook in a small saucepan for 5 minutes.

Mix the cornstarch with cold water. Add it to the sauce and cook until the sauce thickens and clears, stirring frequently. Serve warm with egg rolls. This sauce is also delicious with any tempura dish. Refrigerated, it will keep well for up to one week.

Yield: 1 cup

Noodle Nests with Shrimp

This was dreamt up on a lovely beach in the San Juan Islands north of Seattle when all of our appetites were whetted by the beauty of it all.

1 10-ounce package coil vermicelli
1 teaspoon dark sesame oil

1 cup chicken stock
2 teaspoons sherry
2 teaspoons soy sauce
½ teaspoon salt
¼ teaspoon dark sesame oil
1 teaspoon honey
1 teaspoon grated fresh ginger
dash of hot chili oil (optional)
1½ tablespoons cornstarch
¼ cup cold water
½ pound snow peas, cut in half
1 15-ounce can baby corn, drained
½ pound baby shrimp
3 green onions, diced
oil for frying

In a 2-quart pot, cook the noodles in boiling salted water for 8 minutes. Drain, rinse under cold water, drain again, and sprinkle with 1 teaspoon sesame oil. Spread the noodles out on a cookie sheet to air.

Heat the chicken stock in a 2-quart pot on medium-high heat until it is simmering. Add the sherry, soy sauce, salt, ¼ teaspoon sesame oil, honey, ginger, and optional hot chili oil. Dissolve the cornstarch in cold water and stir it into the sauce. Cook over medium heat for about 3 minutes until the sauce thickens and the cornstarch clears. Add the snow peas, corn, shrimp, and green onions and heat through. Turn off the heat and set aside.

Divide the noodles into 6 equal piles. Form each pile into a pancake shape.

Heat 4 tablespoons of oil in a frying pan over high heat. Press the noodle pancake down in the pan with a spatula to make it hold together and fry it until brown on one side, about 4 minutes. Flip and brown it on the other side for about 2 minutes. Remove and drain on a paper towel. Keep warm in the oven until all of the noodles are done. Add more oil as needed for frying.

Reheat the sauce and serve it over the hot noodle nests.

Yield: 6 servings

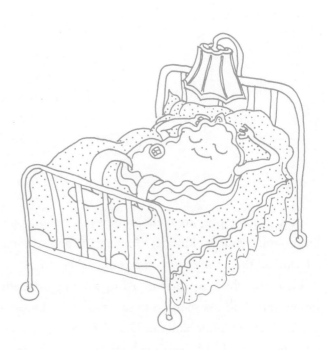

Oysters en Brochette

1 pound whole mushrooms

2 tablespoons butter

2 tablespoons soy sauce

2 tablespoons dry cooking sherry

1 quart raw oysters

1 pound thick-sliced bacon, cut in
  2-inch pieces

½ cup butter, melted

1½ cups seasoned bread crumbs

6 skewers

Cook the mushrooms on high heat with 2 tablespoons butter, soy sauce, and sherry in a large covered pan until the mixture comes to a boil. Drain, reserving the juice for another use.

Drain and pick over the oysters for bits of shell. In a 2-quart saucepan, drop oysters into boiling water to cover. Continue boiling until the oysters plump up and the edges begin to curl, approximately 2 minutes. Drain immediately.

Fry the bacon in a large skillet until limp and starting to brown around the edges. Drain.

String the mushrooms, oysters, and bacon on skewers, beginning and ending with mushrooms. Roll the brochettes in melted butter and dredge them in bread crumbs. Broil until browned, about 8 minutes, turning once. Serve immediately.

Note: If you want to prepare the brochettes ahead of time, follow the process through dredging the skewers in bread crumbs. Refrigerate them until you are ready to broil. These are also delicious barbecued.

Yield: 6 servings

Peasant Greens with Pork

The greens are Swiss chard, which grows in abundance in the Northwest, summer and winter alike. Lemon juice lends a tang to this simple peasant dish. This dish can be made in a flash.

1⅓ pounds pork steak or pork
    butt
2 tablespoons soy sauce
3 tablespoons lemon juice
1 pound new potatoes, sliced
2 to 3 tablespoons olive oil
1 onion, sliced in ¼-inch slices
1 bunch Swiss chard, diced in
    1-inch sections

Slice the pork into ⅛-inch strips and marinate in soy sauce and lemon juice while preparing the remaining ingredients.

Steam the new potatoes, 10 to 15 minutes.

Drain the marinade from the pork and reserve. Heat the oil in a large wok or frying pan. Stir-fry the pork over high heat until the pink color has gone from the meat. Add the onion slices and stir to mix. Top with the prepared greens and juice from the marinade. Cover and steam until the greens are of the desired softness. Serve over the steamed new potatoes.

Yield: 4 to 6 servings

Javanese Rice Table

Judith's sister, Beth, is a world traveller, and one of the best cooks we've had on our staff. She brought this recipe back after a trip to Thailand and Nepal. This spicy chicken-over-rice is accompanied by a choice of condiments and a tangy pineapple chutney. With this special, people have a chance to play with their food, mixing and matching flavors to their liking as they savor the unusual combination of nuts, fruits, pickles, rice, and chicken. The colors, aroma, and flavors are intoxicating.

Brown or White Rice (see
   page 226)

3/4 pound boneless chicken,
   skinned and cubed
1 1/2 teaspoons hot chili oil
2 cloves garlic, minced
1/2 onion, diced
zest of 1 lime, minced
1/2 cup chopped fresh cilantro
1 1/2 teaspoons grated fresh ginger
1/8 teaspoon cardamom
3/4 teaspoon salt
1/2 teaspoon curry powder
1 1/2 teaspoons sugar
1 14-ounce can coconut milk

Pineapple Chutney (page 233)
condiments:
   2 dill pickles, chopped
   1/4 cup raisins
   2 hard-boiled eggs, chopped
   1/4 cup roasted peanuts
   1/4 cup toasted shredded
      coconut

Prepare the rice and keep it hot until you are ready to serve.

In a large saucepan, sauté the cubed chicken in the hot oil until it browns. Then add the garlic and onion. Cook until the onion is transparent. Add the lime zest, cilantro, ginger, cardamom, salt, curry, and sugar. Let cook another

10 minutes, stirring occasionally to keep from sticking. Add the coconut milk. Let simmer another 10 minutes before serving.

To serve, spoon a liberal helping of rice on a deep-dish plate with sides. Cover with the curried chicken and sauce and top with a heaping spoonful of chutney. Surround the chutney with a small helping of each of the condiments.

Yield: 4 servings

Garbanzo Bean and Sesame Seed Curry

We offer this dish as a vegetarian alternative when Javanese Rice Table is on the menu because it goes well with the same condiments and chutney that accompany the Rice Table.

¾ cup dry garbanzo beans
   (2 cups cooked)
2 cups water

Brown or White Rice (see
   page 226)
4 tablespoons olive oil
1 onion, diced
5 cloves garlic, minced
⅓ cup sesame seeds
½ teaspoon coriander seeds
½ teaspoon mustard seeds
½ teaspoon cumin seeds
2 cups fresh or frozen peas
2 stalks lemon grass, chopped
   into 2-inch pieces

2½ cups milk
3 tablespoons unbleached white
   flour
1½ teaspoons salt
½ teaspoon turmeric

Put the garbanzo beans and water in a 2-quart soup pot. Cover and bring to a boil. Lower heat and simmer for 45 minutes. Remove and drain.

Prepare the rice and keep it hot until you are ready to serve.

Heat the oil in a skillet and sauté the onion and garlic until the onion becomes transparent. Set aside.

In a small cast-iron skillet, toast the sesame seeds until they begin popping. Remove and set aside. In the same skillet, toast the coriander, mustard, and cumin seeds until they turn light brown; grind them with a mortar and pestle.

Put the onion and garlic back on medium heat and add the ground spices.

Keep sautéing and add the peas and lemon grass. In a small bowl, whisk the milk, flour, and salt together. Pour it into the onion mixture and cook, stirring constantly, until it thickens. Lower heat. Add the garbanzo beans, turmeric, and sesame seeds, and cook 10 more minutes.

Serve on a bed of rice with Pineapple Chutney (see page 233) and the same condiments offered with Javanese Rice Table (see preceding recipe).

Yield: 4 servings

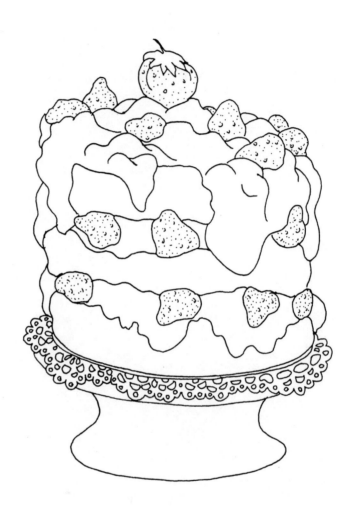

CAKES

Cakes are not a part of the daily dessert fare at the Streamliner Diner, simply because they take a little too much time to prepare and they're hard to fit into the schedule. We make them when time permits or when the inclination arises. Because they are not offered regularly, when we do make a cake, it usually sells out right away.

Our cakes are special occasion items in more sense than one. The Poppy Seed–Lemon–Raspberry Cake was dreamt up for Alexandra's wedding.

Brer Rabbit's Carrot Cake

"Whatever you do, please don't make me eat another piece of that carrot cake!"

2 cups unbleached white flour
2 teaspoons baking powder
1 teaspoon baking soda
1 cup granulated sugar
1 cup brown sugar, packed
1 teaspoon salt
2 teaspoons cinnamon
1 teaspoon cardamom
½ teaspoon nutmeg
1 cup coarsely chopped walnuts

4 eggs
2 cups grated carrots
1 20-ounce can crushed
   pineapple, drained
1 cup vegetable oil
2 teaspoons vanilla
zest of 1 orange, minced

Lemon Cream Cheese Icing (see
   recipe below)

Preheat oven to 350°. Grease and flour two round 9-inch pans.

Thoroughly mix the flour, baking powder, baking soda, granulated and brown sugars, salt, cinnamon, cardamom, nutmeg, and walnuts in a large bowl.

In a medium-sized bowl, beat together the eggs, carrots, pineapple, oil, vanilla, and orange zest. Pour wet mixture into dry mixture. With a large spoon, stir until well mixed. Divide batter between the two cake pans.

Bake at 350° for 45 minutes or until a toothpick inserted in the center comes out clean. Turn the cake upside down on a rack and allow to cool in the pan. Remove the cake from the pan, ice with Lemon–Cream Cheese Icing, and voilà!

Yield: One 9-inch round layer cake

Lemon–Cream Cheese Icing

½ cup butter, softened
1 cup powdered sugar, sifted
16 ounces cream cheese
3 tablespoons lemon juice

In a medium-sized bowl, cream together the butter and powdered sugar with an electric mixer or large spoon until smooth. Beat in the cream cheese until smooth. Mix in lemon juice.

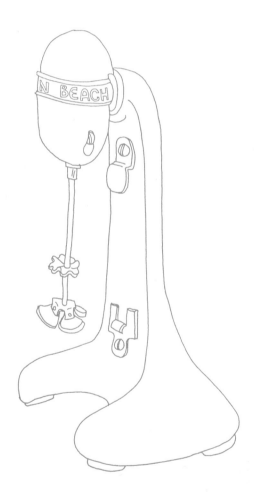

Chocolate Mayonnaise Cake

This is a traditional chocolate cake. It comes out moist and perfect every time. Orion, Alexandra's son, loves this cake, so Judith, his surrogate auntie, indulges him with this every year on his birthday.

3 cups unbleached white flour
1½ cups sugar
⅔ cup unsweetened cocoa
2¼ teaspoons baking powder
1½ teaspoons baking soda
1½ cups water
1½ cups mayonnaise
1½ teaspoons vanilla
optional: zest of 1 orange,
   or 2 tablespoons rum,
   or 1 teaspoon rum
   extract mixed with
   1½ tablespoons water

Chocolate Frosting (see recipe
   opposite)

Preheat oven to 350°. Grease and flour two 9-inch round pans.

In a large bowl, sift together the flour, sugar, cocoa, and baking powder and soda. In another bowl, whisk together the water, mayonnaise, and vanilla (and any one of the optional ingredients) until smooth. Add this to the dry ingredients and mix well. Divide batter between the two cake pans and bake at 350° for 40 minutes.

Remove the cakes from oven and cool them in the pans for 10 minutes. Turn them upside down on cake racks and remove the pans. Allow cakes to completely cool before frosting.

Yield: One 9-inch round layer cake

Chocolate Frosting

2 ounces unsweetened baker's
  chocolate
1 cup butter, room temperature
½ cup sour cream
4 cups sifted powdered sugar
1 teaspoon vanilla

In a small pan, melt chocolate in a 350° oven or in a double boiler on top of the stove, and set aside to cool.

With an electric mixer, cream butter until light and fluffy. Add sour cream and continue to beat until combined. Add sugar, a little at a time, continuing to beat until smooth. Add vanilla and melted chocolate. Mix thoroughly.

Jones's Orange Chocolate Cake

A friend of Irene's named Gerry Jones generously gave us his family's favorite cake recipe. This cake has a rich chocolate flavor with a hint of orange for adventure. Thanks to the Jones family for the greatest orange chocolate cake imaginable.

½ cup butter	1 teaspoon salt
1 cup granulated sugar	2 cups unbleached white flour, sifted
1 cup brown sugar, packed	
3 eggs, separated	1 teaspoon baking soda
zest and juice of 1 orange	1 teaspoon baking powder
1 teaspoon vanilla	1 cup buttermilk

½ cup unsweetened cocoa
½ cup boiling water

Preheat oven to 350°. Grease and flour two 9-inch round pans.

In a large bowl, cream the butter with an electric mixer until soft. Add the sugars and beat until light and fluffy. Add 3 egg yolks, and continue to beat until the mixture is light yellow in color. Beat in the orange zest and juice and vanilla.

In a small bowl, make a paste with the cocoa and boiling water. Add to the batter and beat until thoroughly incorporated.

Beat the 3 egg whites with salt until stiff. Set aside.

Sift together the flour, baking soda, and baking powder in a separate bowl. Add half the dry ingredients to the batter alternately with half the buttermilk, stirring after each addition until all is combined. Fold in the egg whites with a rubber spatula using as few strokes as possible. Pour the batter into the pans.

Bake at 350° for 30 minutes until a toothpick inserted in the middle comes out clean. Cool the cakes in the pans for 10 minutes. Turn them upside down on cake racks and remove the pans. When thoroughly cool, ice the cake with your favorite frosting, or use the Chocolate Frosting on page 193.

Yield: One 9-inch round layer cake

Four–Layer German Chocolate Cake

This is the Streamliner's rich, moist version of German Chocolate Cake. We make it with delicious Toffee Nut Icing.

¾ cup butter	3 cups unbleached white flour
1½ cups sugar	1 tablespoon baking powder
4 eggs, separated	½ teaspoon salt
2 teaspoons vanilla	
4 ounces unsweetened baker's chocolate, melted and cooled	1½ cups buttermilk
	Toffee Nut Icing (see recipe opposite)

Preheat oven to 350°. Grease and flour two 9-inch round cake pans.

In a large mixing bowl, cream the butter with an electric mixer until light and fluffy. Slowly add the sugar while continuing to cream, and beat until the mixture is light yellow in color. Add the egg yolks, one at a time, beating after each addition. Add the vanilla and chocolate and stir to combine.

Sift the flour with the baking powder and salt. Alternately add the buttermilk and the flour to the batter, a little at a time, beating until all of the ingredients are blended together.

In another mixing bowl, beat the egg whites until stiff. Fold the egg whites into the cake batter with as few strokes as possible.

Pour the batter into the pans and bake at 350° for 25 minutes, or until a toothpick inserted in the middle comes out clean. Remove from the oven and cool 10 minutes. Remove the cakes from the pans. Cut each cake horizontally in half, and set aside.

Yield: One 9-inch round layer cake

Toffee Nut Icing

4 egg yolks

1 cup sugar

1 12-ounce can evaporated milk

2 teaspoons vanilla

1/4 cup butter

2 cups shredded coconut

2 cups chopped walnuts

In a medium-sized stainless steel saucepan, beat 4 egg yolks with a wire whisk until they are light yellow. Whisk in the sugar, evaporated milk, and vanilla, in that order, making sure each ingredient is fully incorporated before the next addition.

Put the icing on medium-high heat, stirring constantly, until it begins to bubble and thicken. Lower the heat and continue stirring and cooking for 3 more minutes. Add the butter and remove from heat, stirring until the butter is melted. Refrigerate for 30 minutes.

Stir in the coconut and walnuts.

Starting with the bottom layer, ice each of the four layers with a thin layer of the Toffee Nut Icing until you have a four-layer cake. Do not ice the sides.

Poppy Seed–Lemon–Raspberry Cake

This was Alexandra's wedding cake. We multiplied the recipe by eight and made a three-tiered cake, beautifully decorated by Irene. We filled the first tier with vanilla custard, and the second and third tiers with raspberries. If you need to make a wedding cake, this works beautifully.

½ cup poppy seeds
1 cup half-and-half (milk works, too)

12 ounces fresh or frozen raspberries, mashed
whipping cream

¾ cup butter
1½ cups sugar
4 eggs, separated
1½ teaspoons vanilla
1 tablespoon lemon zest, minced
2 cups unbleached white flour
2½ teaspoons baking powder
½ teaspoon salt

Preheat oven to 350°. Grease two 10-inch round cake pans.

Soak the poppy seeds in half-and-half for 30 minutes.

With an electric mixer, cream the butter until soft in a medium-sized mixing bowl. Continue creaming the butter while adding the sugar in a steady stream. Beat until the mixture is fluffy and light yellow in color. Add the egg yolks, one at a time, fully incorporating each one before adding the next. Stir in the vanilla, poppy seeds and half-and-half, and lemon zest, allowing each ingredient to become thoroughly mixed into the batter before adding the next.

In another mixing bowl, sift the flour, baking powder, and salt together. Add it to the batter slowly, beating continuously.

In a small mixing bowl, beat the egg whites until stiff. Fold them into the cake batter with as few strokes as possible. Pour the batter into the cake pans.

Bake at 350° for 45 to 50 minutes. Remove from the oven and cool cakes in the pans. Remove cakes from pans. Spread the mashed raspberries between the layers. Serve with whipped cream.

Yield: One 10-inch round layer cake

Tollhouse Shortbread Bars

These chocolate chip bars layered with coconut and shortbread are popular among chocolate lovers. In the spring of 1990, we created this recipe for the Seattle Folk Life Festival, where they were a hot-selling item. People kept returning for more. These bars freeze well. They are fairly easy to make and would be great to take to a potluck or a large family gathering.

1 cup butter	1/2 cup butter
1/2 cup packed brown sugar	2 eggs
2 cups unbleached white flour	1/4 cup granulated sugar
1/4 teaspoon salt	1/3 cup packed brown sugar
1/4 teaspoon baking powder	3/4 cup unbleached white flour
1 cup shredded coconut	1 1/2 cups semisweet chocolate chips
	1 cup chopped walnuts

Preheat oven to 350°. Grease a 10 × 15-inch baking sheet.

To make the shortbread, whip 1 cup butter in a small mixing bowl with an electric mixer until light and fluffy. Cream in 1/2 cup brown sugar.

In a medium-sized bowl, sift together the 2 cups of flour, salt, and baking powder. Add the creamed butter and stir until the dough is crumbly in texture. Press the dough onto the greased baking sheet, patting it evenly over the entire sheet. Sprinkle the coconut on top of the shortbread.

To make the top layer, melt 1/2 cup butter. Set aside to cool. In a medium-sized mixing bowl, cream together the eggs, granulated sugar, 1/3 cup brown sugar, and the melted butter with the electric mixer. Beat in 3/4 cup flour. Stir in the chocolate chips and walnuts and mix until the ingredients are evenly dispersed. You now have a very sticky batter.

Drop the sticky batter in large spoonfuls all over the shortbread and then with wet hands spread the batter until there is an even layer of chocolate chip mix covering the shortbread.

Bake at 350° for 25 to 30 minutes. Cut into bars while still warm.

Yield: 12 large or 24 small bars

PIES

In Pie We Crust reads our pie board, which always boasts a choice of eight to ten homemade pies. There are the ever-present Peanut Butter Pie and Toll-house Pie, as well as luscious cream and fruit pies.

In the spring and summer we enjoy a lot of freedom as the fruit parade marches by. First come the strawberries and the rhubarb. Close on their heels are the cherries, followed by nectarines, peaches, raspberries, and blackberries. As we move into autumn, the harvest provides us with apples, plums, and pears. All of these grow abundantly in Washington State.

Most of our pies are rich and decadent—definitely dessert stuff, although some people like warmed-up Mile High Apple Pie for breakfast. We keep freshly whipped cream on hand at all times for our customers who desire their pie *à la crème*. All of our pies are deep-dish, made in ten-inch pie plates. This makes impressive, lofty pieces of pie that look just like Grandma's. For the cookbook, we scaled down some of our recipes to nine-inch pies. They'll still look impressive!

Peanut Butter Pie

This pie deserves to be in the *Who's Who of Contemporary American Pies*. Creamy and rich, it is unbeatable when you're in the mood for peanut butter or chocolate. It has been on the menu since the Streamliner Diner first opened its doors, and its popularity is unsurpassed by any other pie we make. For a decadent variation, try the Heavenly Kahlua Cream Pie.

1 Graham Cracker Crust, prebaked (see page 221)

Julie's Chocolate Sauce (see recipe opposite)

1 cup cream cheese
1 cup peanut butter
1 cup sugar
1 teaspoon vanilla
1 cup whipping cream

Prepare the graham cracker pie shell and let it cool.

Whip the cream cheese, peanut butter, sugar, and vanilla together with an electric mixer until fluffy and well blended.

In a separate small bowl, whip the whipping cream until stiff. Fold the whipped cream into the peanut butter mixture. Pour into the pie shell and chill for 2 hours.

Drizzle the chocolate sauce on top. Chill another 2 hours before serving.

Yield: One 9-inch pie

VARIATION

To make Heavenly Kahlua Cream Pie, follow the instructions for Peanut Butter Pie, omitting the peanut butter. Increase the cream cheese to 2½ cups and add ⅓ cup Kahlua or other coffee liqueur at the same time as the vanilla. Drizzle chocolate sauce on top. Refrigerate 4 to 6 hours before serving.

Julie's Chocolate Sauce

⅓ cup half-and-half or whipping
  cream
⅔ cup semisweet chocolate chips
2 tablespoons butter, softened

In a small saucepan, scald the half-and-half or whipping cream. Remove from heat. Stir in the chocolate chips until melted. Add the butter and cook on low heat, stirring until smooth.

Mile High Apple Pie

This pie is unsurpassed in its ability to make mouths water. The pie is mounded high and looms over our counter like Mt. Rainier looms over the shore of Puget Sound, eliciting appreciative "ooohs" and "aaahs."

2 recipes Pie Crust, unbaked (see page 219)

Brown sugar separates from butter

10 large apples
1 cup butter
½ cup unbleached white flour
zest of 1 lemon, minced
1 cup packed brown sugar or honey
1 tablespoon cinnamon
½ teaspoon salt
1 egg, beaten

Preheat oven to 350°. Prepare a double recipe of pie dough. On a lightly floured surface, roll out half the dough with a rolling pin and place it in the pie pan. Leave the other half for the top crust.

Peel, core, and slice the apples in thin wedges. Place them in a large bowl and set aside.

In a medium-sized saucepan, melt the butter on low heat. Add the flour and stir, using a wire whisk. Let cook 2 minutes. Whisk in the lemon zest, sugar or honey, cinnamon, and salt. Let cook another 2 to 3 minutes. Pour onto the apples and mix in thoroughly. Spoon the apples into the pie shell.

Roll out the top pie crust. Cover the pie and crimp the edges. Cut slits in the top crust or poke with a fork to allow steam to escape while baking. Brush the top of the pie with the beaten egg.

Bake at 350° for 1 hour and 15 minutes, or until the crust is deep golden brown and the juices have thickened and are oozing out of the top of the pie.

Yield: One 10-inch pie

Berry Fresh Pie

A bite of this fresh pie is reward enough for the stained fingers, bug bites, torn clothing, and blazing sun endured while collecting the berries.

1 recipe Pie Crust, prebaked (see page 219)

8 ounces cream cheese
¼ cup sugar
1 cup whipping cream

4½ tablespoons cornstarch
5 cups blueberries
1 cup sugar
pinch of salt
1 cup cold water
3 tablespoons butter
zest and juice of 1 lemon

Prepare the pie shell and let it cool.

In a saucepan, mix the cornstarch with 2½ cups of the berries, 1 cup sugar, and salt. Stir in the water. Bring to a boil and cook over medium heat. Stir frequently until thick, about 7 minutes. Remove from heat. Stir in the butter and lemon zest and juice, and let cool. When cool, add the remaining berries.

With an electric mixer, whip the cream cheese with ¼ cup sugar in a medium-sized bowl. In another bowl, whip the whipping cream until stiff and fold it into the cream cheese. Spread this mixture over the bottom of the cooled pie shell. Pour the berry mixture on top, filling the pie shell. Refrigerate for a few hours until set.

Yield: One 10-inch pie

VARIATION

Substitute strawberries, blackberries, or raspberries for the blueberries.

Strawberry Rhubarb Crumb Pie

If you are a strawberry or a rhubarb fan, you will love this pie!

1 recipe Pie Crust, unbaked (see
page 219)

Crumb Topping (see page 222)

1 pound rhubarb (4 cups)
1 pound strawberries (3 cups)
¾ cup sugar
2 tablespoons tapioca

Prepare the pie shell. Preheat oven to 350°.

Slice the rhubarb in ¾-inch pieces. Slice the strawberries. Place the fruit in a large mixing bowl. Add the sugar and tapioca and mix thoroughly. Set aside for 15 minutes. Pour into pie shell.

Bake at 350° for 20 minutes. While the pie is baking, prepare the crumb topping.

After 20 minutes, sprinkle the crumb topping onto the pie and return it to the oven to bake for another 40 to 50 minutes, until the top begins to brown and the fruit is bubbling.

Yield: One 9-inch pie

Tollhouse Pie

This is like a big, rich, chocolate chip–butter toffee bar. Watch out!

1 recipe Pie Crust, unbaked (see
   page 219)

¾ cup butter
3 eggs
¾ cup granulated sugar
1 cup brown sugar, packed
1 cup unbleached white flour
2 cups semisweet chocolate chips
1½ cups chopped walnuts

Prepare the pie shell. Preheat oven to 350°.

In a small saucepan, melt the butter. Set aside to cool.

In a medium-sized bowl, beat the eggs with an electric mixer. Add the sugars and flour, continuing to beat until the mixture is light and creamy. Beat in the cooled butter until thoroughly incorporated. Stir in the chocolate chips and walnuts with a mixing spoon. Pour the filling into the pie shell.

Bake at 350° for 45 minutes. Cool before serving.

Yield: One 10-inch pie

Julie's Chocolate Caramel Pie

Julie Clifford created this outrageous dessert, one slice of which will completely satisfy the fiercest of chocolate cravings.

1 Graham Cracker Crust,
  prebaked (see page 221)

3 cups semisweet chocolate chips
½ cup sugar
1 pound cream cheese
2 cups whipping cream

15 caramels
2 to 3 tablespoons milk or cream

Prepare the pie shell and let it cool.

Melt the chocolate chips over low heat in a double boiler, or in a slow oven, and set aside.

In a medium-sized bowl, with an electric mixer, cream together the sugar and cream cheese until light and fluffy. Add the melted chocolate and mix until thoroughly blended.

In a small mixing bowl, whip the cream. Fold the whipped cream into the cream cheese mixture, until all the white disappears. Spoon the filling into the cooled pie shell.

In a small saucepan, over a low heat, stir the caramels into the milk until they dissolve into a sauce consistency. Remove from heat. Drizzle the topping over the pie. Chill before serving.

Yield: One 10-inch pie

Streamliner Cheese Cake Pie

1 Graham Cracker Crust,
   unbaked (see page 221)

19 ounces cream cheese, room
   temperature
½ cup sugar
4 eggs
1 tablespoon lemon juice
1 teaspoon vanilla
pinch of salt

1 cup sour cream
3½ tablespoons sugar
½ teaspoon vanilla

Prepare the Graham Cracker Crust. Preheat oven to 300°.

Beat the cream cheese and ½ cup sugar with an electric mixer until creamy and smooth. Add the eggs, one at a time, beating well after each addition. Add the lemon juice, vanilla, and salt. Beat until smooth. Pour the filling into the pie crust and bake at 300° for 30 minutes or until set and lightly browned on top. Remove from the oven and cool slightly.

Mix together the sour cream, 3½ tablespoons sugar, and vanilla. Spread this over the cream cheese filling. Chill for 4 hours before serving.

Yield: One 9-inch pie

VARIATION

For a Chocolate–Almond–Cream Cheese Pie, combine the cream cheese with 4 ounces melted unsweetened baker's chocolate and increase the sugar to 1 cup. Substitute 1 teaspoon almond extract for the lemon juice and vanilla. Sprinkle ¼ cup toasted chopped almonds on top of the sour cream frosting.

Lemon Meringue Pie

1 recipe Pie Crust, prebaked (see
   page 219)

2½ cups water
1¼ cups sugar
½ cup cornstarch

5 eggs, separated
½ cup lemon juice
1 tablespoon lemon zest, minced
¼ cup butter

5 egg whites
1½ cups sugar

Prepare the pie shell and let it cool.

In a small saucepan, bring the water to a boil. In another small saucepan, mix 1¼ cups sugar and cornstarch with a wire whisk. Pour the boiling water over the sugar and cornstarch, stirring with the whisk constantly to avoid lumping. Return to low heat and cook, stirring constantly, until the cornstarch clears. Cover, and let cook another 3 minutes. It will be thick and glutinous.

In a small mixing bowl, whisk 5 egg yolks. Set aside the egg whites for the meringue. Pour half of the sugar filling over the yolks and whisk until it is well blended. Stir this back into the rest of the filling. Cook another 2 minutes and turn off the heat. Stir in the lemon juice and zest until fully incorporated. Stir in the butter until it is fully melted and incorporated. Pour the filling into the pie shell and set aside until the meringue is done.

Preheat the oven to 400°. To make the meringue, take the 5 egg whites left over from the pie filling, add 5 more egg whites, and begin whipping them in a medium-sized mixing bowl with an electric mixer. When they begin to thin and look frothy, start adding 1½ cups sugar in a slow, steady stream, whipping continuously, until the meringue forms stiff peaks.

Spread the meringue onto the lemon filling with a rubber spatula, making sure the meringue touches the edges of the crust, otherwise both you and the pie will end up weeping. Brown the meringue in the oven. This will only take a couple of minutes. Remove from the oven and chill in the refrigerator for at least 4 to 6 hours before serving.

Yield: One 10-inch pie

Honey Pumpkin Pie

This pie is simple to make—easy as pie, as the saying goes.

1 recipe Pie Crust, unbaked (see
    page 219)

1 29-ounce can pumpkin purée,
    or 3 1/2 cups cooked pumpkin
    purée
4 eggs, beaten
3/4 cup milk
3/4 cup honey
1/8 teaspoon salt
1 teaspoon vanilla
1 teaspoon cinnamon
1/4 teaspoon nutmeg
1/8 teaspoon ground cloves

whipped cream

Prepare the pie shell. Preheat oven to 375°.

In a large bowl or food processor, beat together the pumpkin purée, eggs, milk, honey, salt, vanilla, cinnamon, nutmeg, and cloves. Pour it into the unbaked shell.

Bake at 375° for 55 minutes or until a knife inserted in the center of the pie comes out clean. Serve warm or cold with fresh whipped cream.

Note: If you would like to make your own pumpkin purée, cut the pumpkin into large chunks and steam in a steamer or boil in water to cover until very tender. Remove from pot, peel, and mash.

Yield: One 9-inch pie

Pumpkin Brandy Pie

When it comes 'round to the holiday season, we like to try brandy in just about everything. This is a lovely way to enhance pumpkin pie.

1 Graham Cracker Crust, prebaked (see page 221)

¾ cup whipping cream

1¾ cups canned pumpkin purée

20 ounces cream cheese

1 cup sugar

⅓ cup brandy

zest of 1 orange, minced

Prepare the pie crust and let it cool.

In a medium-sized bowl, with an electric mixer, whip the cream cheese until it is light and fluffy. Continue whipping and add the sugar slowly until it is fully incorporated. Beat in the brandy and orange zest.

In a small mixing bowl, whip the cream until stiff. Fold the pumpkin purée into the whipped cream. Fold that mixture into the cream cheese mixture. Turn the filling into the Graham Cracker Crust. Refrigerate 4 to 6 hours before serving.

Yield: One 10-inch pie

Vanilla Cream Pie

1 recipe Pie Crust, prebaked (see page 219)

4 cups milk
2 cups sugar
6 tablespoons cornstarch
6 egg yolks

3 tablespoons butter or margarine
1 teaspoon vanilla

1 1-ounce package gelatin
¼ cup cold water

Prepare the pie shell and let it cool.

Heat the milk slowly in a heavy-bottomed 2-quart saucepan. In a small bowl, mix together the sugar and cornstarch. Add it to the milk and cook over medium heat, stirring frequently, until the mixture thickens and starts to bubble. Cook for 3 minutes, stirring constantly. Turn the heat down as low as possible.

In a small bowl, beat the egg yolks with a wire whisk. Add a small amount of the hot milk to the yolks, whisk, and add it all back to the pot. Cook over low heat for 2 more minutes. Remove the custard from heat and stir in the butter or margarine and vanilla.

Dissolve the gelatin in the water and stir it into the custard. Immediately pour the filling into the pie shell. Chill for at least 3 hours before serving.

Yield: One 10-inch pie

VARIATIONS

- To make Chocolate Cream Pie, add 4 ounces melted unsweetened baker's chocolate to the custard at the same time that you add the butter or margarine and vanilla.

- To make Banana Cream Pie, slice 3 bananas and make a layer of the banana slices in the bottom of the prebaked pie shell before pouring in the vanilla custard.

■ For Coconut Cream Pie, mix in 1 teaspoon almond extract and ¾ cup toasted, shredded coconut to the custard. Pour the filling into the pie shell and sprinkle another ¼ cup of the toasted coconut over the top of the pie.

Eggnog Pie

This is Judith's cure for the midwinter blues. Speaking strictly as Northwesterners, there's nothing better on a rainy Christmas Day.

1 Graham Cracker Crust, prebaked (see page 221)

3 ounces unsweetened baker's chocolate

1 1-ounce package gelatin

¼ cup cold water

½ cup sugar

4 tablespoons cornstarch

4 egg yolks

4 cups eggnog

¼ cup brandy

¼ cup rum

Prepare the pie crust and let it cool.

In a double boiler, melt the chocolate. Pour it into a small mixing bowl, and set aside to cool.

Dissolve the gelatin in cold water. Set aside.

Clean the double boiler and, with a wire whisk, mix the sugar and cornstarch in the pan. Whisk in one egg yolk at a time until they are thoroughly incorporated and the mixture is thick and light yellow in color. Whisk in the eggnog. Put the double boiler on high heat to cook the custard, stirring occasionally to keep it from sticking. When the custard begins to bubble, cook for 5 more minutes. Remove from heat. Stir in the gelatin.

Ladle 2 cups of the custard into the chocolate. Add the brandy and stir until the mixture is smooth.

Stir the rum into the rest of the custard. Pour the rum custard into the pie shell. Pour the chocolate custard evenly over the entire pie, making sure not to pour too much in any one area. Smooth it out with a rubber spatula until it covers the top of the pie to the edges. Refrigerate 4 to 6 hours before serving.

Yield: One 10-inch pie

Pie Crust

The Streamliner's secret method for making flaky pie dough is to use chopsticks to mix the dough. This prevents overhandling, the principal culprit responsible for tough pie crusts.

⅓ cup cold butter or margarine (¾ stick)	1⅓ cups unbleached white flour
	6 tablespoons ice water

Put the butter or margarine and flour in a medium-sized bowl, and cut it with a pastry blender until a uniform crumb is formed. Using a pair of chopsticks, work the cold water into the flour, a few drops at a time. Stir in a small circular motion until clumps of dough form. Push clumps aside and move on to

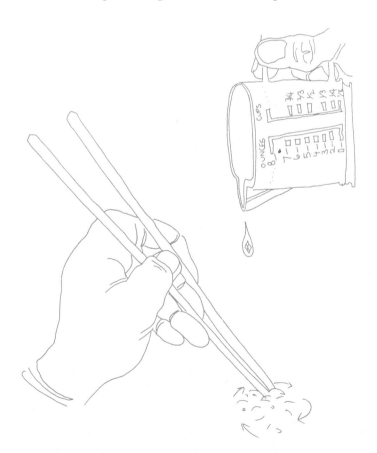

the next area. Continue to add drops of water while mixing until all of the water has been incorporated and the whole mixture consists of one large clump of dough. If you are using a food processor, put the flour in the processor bowl. Cut the butter or margarine into small chunks, add it to the bowl, and pulse 11 times.

With as little handling as possible, form the dough into a ball using the palms of your hands. Flatten the ball slightly. Wrap in plastic wrap and refrigerate for 1 hour or until needed. This dough will keep refrigerated for several days.

To prepare a pie crust, roll the dough on a lightly floured surface. Carefully place it in a 9- or 10-inch pie pan. Fold edges under and crimp.

For a prebaked pie shell, prepare the crust. Prick the dough all over with a fork and be sure to crimp the edge of the dough slightly over the lip of the pie plate to prevent the shell from shrinking. Bake in an oven preheated to 375° for 15 minutes or until crust is golden brown. Another method for preventing shrinkage is to set a 9-inch round cake pan in the middle of the pie shell. Bake the crust for half of the total baking time, then remove the cake pan and finish baking.

For a double-crusted pie, double the recipe.

Yield: One 9- or 10-inch pie shell

Graham Cracker Crust

2 cups graham cracker crumbs

¼ cup sugar

½ teaspoon cinnamon (optional)

10 tablespoons butter or
   margarine, melted

Preheat oven to 400°. In a medium-sized bowl, mix graham cracker crumbs, sugar, and optional cinnamon. Add melted butter or margarine and mix well.

With a fork or using your fingers, press the crumb mixture into a 9- or 10-inch pie plate, building up the sides and smoothing out the edges so that the crust is even.

Bake at 400° for 8 to 10 minutes.

Yield: One 9- or 10-inch pie crust

Crumb Topping

½ cup brown sugar, packed
½ cup unbleached white flour
½ teaspoon cinnamon
¼ cup cold butter
¼ cup finely chopped walnuts

In a small bowl, combine the brown sugar, flour, and cinnamon. Cut in the butter, using a pastry cutter, until the crumb texture is coarse. Stir in the walnuts.

Yield: 1½ cups, enough for 1 pie or coffee cake

À LA CARTE

This chapter is a melting pot of recipes that could not find homes anywhere else. Some of these recipes are accompaniments to those found in other chapters and some are just difficult to classify.

Most of these recipes have earned multiple-use status, that is, you'll find that we use them in many different combinations. Use them with our recipes or with your own. For instance, try the Basic Italian Tomato Sauce (see page 228) on pizza. And what about Pineapple Chutney (see page 233) on a Curried Chicken Salad (see page 126) pocket sandwich?

If you need instructions on making a good pot of rice or if you're expecting guests and want a guacamole dip or salsa for chips, you've turned to the right chapter.

Rice

We serve brown or white rice with so many of our specials, it's almost as much a staple as bread or potatoes. If you like, you can even substitute it for the polenta in Hunter's Stew (see page 166) or Stuffed Tomatoes over Polenta (see page 140). Any leftover rice can be stored in a covered container in the refrigerator for about four days. Reheat it in a steamer or microwave oven. You can also heat it in a little butter in a frying pan.

> 2 cups brown or white rice
> 2¼ cups water

Wash the rice in 3 or 4 changes of water until the water looks clear. Put the rice and 2¼ cups water in a 1½-quart pot with a tight-fitting lid. Cover and bring to a boil, then reduce heat to the lowest setting. For white rice, simmer for 15 minutes, remove pan from heat, and let the rice cook in its own steam 15 more minutes, never removing the lid during this process. For brown rice, add a pinch of salt to the water, cover, and bring to a boil. Reduce the heat to the lowest setting and simmer for 40 minutes.

Use chopsticks or a fork to fluff up the rice.

Yield: 5 to 6 cups

Polenta

Serve hot polenta as a grain dish, topped with freshly grated Parmesan cheese, or use it in one of the various specials that call for it. Cubed leftover polenta is a tasty addition to soup. Leftover polenta can also be fried.

> 3½ cups water
> 1 teaspoon salt
> 2 cloves garlic, minced
> 2 tablespoons butter or margarine
> 1 cup polenta

In a heavy 1½-quart pan bring the water to a boil. Add the salt, garlic, and butter or margarine. Lower the heat and stir in the polenta with a wire whisk. Continue stirring until the polenta has thickened, about 5 minutes. Cover. Cook on low heat for 20 to 30 minutes, stirring occasionally to prevent sticking.

Yield: 3½ cups

Basic Italian Tomato Sauce

This sauce is nothing like the one that Irene's grandmother made when she first came to the United States. Her sauce was a simple mixture of tomato paste and hot water. Irene takes advantage of the herbs and spices now available and puts all sorts of ingredients in her tomato sauce, ingredients that her grandmother could not obtain. This sauce makes any dish calling for an Italian tomato sauce sing "Oy Vey Maria."

We use this sauce in many of our specials. It's a great spaghetti and pizza sauce, too. It will keep refrigerated for about a week. If you freeze it, it will keep even longer.

1 onion, diced	$1/8$ teaspoon pepper
$1/4$ cup olive oil	pinch of ground cloves
2 cloves garlic, minced	$1/8$ teaspoon fennel seeds
2 $14^1/2$-ounce cans whole tomatoes	1 teaspoon grated lemon zest
1 6-ounce can tomato paste	1 teaspoon oregano
1 tablespoon red wine vinegar	1 teaspoon marjoram
1 tablespoon sugar or honey	$1/2$ teaspoon thyme
1 teaspoon salt	1 bay leaf

In a large heavy-bottomed pot, sauté the onion in oil until transparent. Add the remaining ingredients. Stir to combine and simmer for 30 minutes, stirring occasionally. Remove the bay leaf.

Yield: 4 cups

Pesto

A small amount of pesto can add a lot of flavor to many types of dishes, such as pastas, breads, soups, and casseroles. Pesto can be made ahead of time and stored in the refrigerator for a few weeks. It freezes well too. Small servings can be individually frozen in the form of ice cubes. Simply freeze in ice cube trays, pop out, and bag in the freezer for convenient use on a busy day.

1 cup (packed) fresh basil leaves	*½ cup olive oil*
4 cloves garlic	*2 tablespoons lemon juice*
½ cup walnuts or pine nuts	*1 cup grated Parmesan cheese*
	salt to taste (optional)

Purée the basil leaves in a blender or food processor. Continue blending, adding garlic and nuts until they are well ground. Slowly add the olive oil, lemon juice, and Parmesan cheese. Add salt if you desire.

Yield: 1¾ cups

Streamliner Salsa

We serve our homemade salsa with all our Tex-Mex dishes. It's also good as a dip with tortilla chips. For those who like things nice and hot, simply increase the amount of jalapeños. The salsa can be refrigerated for a week.

$\frac{1}{4}$ white onion, minced

2 green onions, minced

1 tablespoon minced cilantro

2 teaspoons minced jalapeños

$1\frac{1}{2}$ cups diced fresh tomatoes, or

    1 $14\frac{1}{2}$-ounce can tomatoes

$\frac{1}{4}$ teaspoon cumin

$\frac{1}{4}$ teaspoon salt

1 teaspoon red wine vinegar

Combine all ingredients, including most of the juice from the tomatoes, if canned. Mix well to blend flavors.

Yield: 2 cups

Refried Beans

We serve our refried beans in Breakfast Burritos (see page 58), and Streamliner Huevos Rancheros (see page 57). They can be refrigerated for several days and reheated in a skillet.

1¼ cups dry pinto beans
2½ cups water

1 tablespoon olive oil
1 small onion, minced
1 clove garlic, minced

2 ounces canned diced green chilies
½ teaspoon salt
1 tablespoon Worcestershire sauce
1 teaspoon soy sauce
¼ teaspoon oregano
1 teaspoon cumin

Rinse the pinto beans well and soak them overnight in 2½ cups water. Drain. Put them in a 2-quart saucepan in water to cover. Bring the beans to a boil. Lower heat, cover, and simmer for 1 hour, or until beans are tender. Add more water if necessary. (If you don't have the time to soak the beans overnight, a quick method is to bring beans and water to a boil in a 2-quart saucepan, turn off heat, cover, and allow to soak for an hour.)

Mash the beans with a potato masher or blend in a food processor.

In a small frying pan, heat the olive oil over high heat. Sauté the onion and garlic, stirring frequently, until the onion is transparent. Remove from heat. Mix in the green chilies, salt, Worcestershire sauce, soy sauce, oregano, and cumin. Combine all with the beans.

Yield: 3 cups

Guacamole

Guacamole is best freshly made, but can be refrigerated and served the following day.

2 ripe avocadoes
4 tablespoons Streamliner Salsa
    (see page 230)
juice of 1/2 lemon
1/4 teaspoon salt
1 tablespoon sour cream
1/2 teaspoon cumin

Scoop out the avocadoes and mash them with a potato masher or fork. Mix together the avocadoes with the salsa, lemon juice, salt, sour cream, and cumin.

Yield: 1 1/2 cups

Pineapple Chutney

You can use any fruit or vegetable to make a chutney. Some of our favorite kinds are mango, kiwi, tamarind, and green apple. Other more unique ones we have made are green pepper and tomato chutneys. You simply make a "relish" with a fruit or vegetable and vinegar, sugar, garlic, ginger, and lime or lemon zest. Once you have acquired a taste for chutney you will enjoy it on just about any meat, grain, or poultry dish.

1 cup chopped fresh or canned
   pineapple
1 cup apple cider vinegar
½ cup brown sugar
5 cloves garlic, minced
¼ cup grated fresh ginger
½ teaspoon coriander seeds
2 teaspoons grated lemon zest
½ teaspoon salt

Put all the ingredients in a small saucepan on medium-high heat. When it begins to boil, lower the heat and simmer until the juices begin to thicken and become syrupy, approximately 30 minutes. Remove from heat and let cool. The chutney will thicken and have a relish consistency. Refrigerate if you are not going to serve immediately.

Yield: 1 cup

Pâté des Bois
(Mushroom Pâté)

Our forest friend, the mushroom, lends itself beautifully to this pâté. It is luscious on crackers for hors d'oeuvres.

- 1½ pounds domestic or wild
  mushrooms (see note below)
- 3 tablespoons butter
- 3 cloves garlic, minced
- 2 tablespoons lemon juice
- 3 tablespoons anchovy paste, or
  15 anchovy fillets
- ¼ teaspoon pepper
- 1 teaspoon Worcestershire sauce

Finely chop the mushrooms. Sauté them in butter and garlic until all of the juices have evaporated. Blend the mushrooms, lemon juice, anchovy paste or fillets, pepper, and Worcestershire sauce in a food processor until the mixture is smooth. Chill overnight in a bowl or a mold. Serve at room temperature.

Note: If wild mushrooms are used, they will be higher in water content and will need to be cooked longer for the water to evaporate. Each species of wild edible mushroom has its own distinct flavor. The edible species of *Agaricus*, *Boletus*, and *tricholoma* are good for this pâté. Only experienced mushroom hunters should venture to gather and eat wild mushrooms as there are many that are poisonous and even deadly.

Yield: 2¼ cups

Smoked Salmon Spread

Streamliner Smoked Salmon and Bagel Platter is served as a weekend special for patrons who want a taste of the Northwest. Our platter includes the salmon spread on a steamed or toasted Streamliner Bagel (see page 83), thick slices of tomato, paper-thin slivers of red onion, a tiny cup of capers, and fruit for garnish.

8 ounces cream cheese, room
    temperature
4 ounces smoked salmon
2 tablespoons lemon juice
1 tablespoon capers
1/2 teaspoon dried dill weed
1/4 teaspoon pepper

In a medium-sized bowl, beat the cream cheese with an electric mixer until smooth and fluffy.

Flake apart the smoked salmon with your fingers, being careful to remove bones and skin. Add the salmon, lemon juice, capers, dill weed, and pepper to the cream cheese and mix well. Store in a covered container in the refrigerator until ready to serve. This keeps refrigerated for up to 1 week.

Yield: 1½ cups

Fried Apple Rings

3 eggs, lightly beaten
1⅓ cups milk
1 tablespoon butter, melted
1 cup unbleached white flour
½ teaspoon salt

3 tart green apples, peeled, cored, and sliced into ¼-inch rings
butter for frying

½ cup sugar
1 teaspoon cinnamon

With a wire whisk, blend together eggs, milk, and butter in a small mixing bowl. In another small bowl, sift the flour and salt together. Add it to the eggs and milk. Stir in until well blended. Refrigerate for 1 hour.

Dip apple rings into the batter. Fry in a skillet, in a small amount of butter over medium heat, until tender and brown on both sides. Stack on a platter.

Combine the sugar and cinnamon. Sprinkle the apples with cinnamon sugar. Serve hot.

Yield: 3 to 4 servings

INDEX